Stars Join Forces for Relief Aid (9/22)
Kids Do Their Part to Help After Attack (9/26)
Donations Still Pouring In (9/26)
Kin, Co-Workers Honor Windows Victims (10/2)
Generous Act by Film Star (10/2)
Donations Haven't Tapered Off (10/3)
Across Area, Proud & Loving Tributes for Terror Victims (10/3)
Y's Work During Crisis Brings Help From Afar (10/5)
972 Oregonians Fly Here 'Cuz They Love N.Y. (10/7)
Restaurants Aid Victims' Kin (10/11)
Help Comes in Cupfuls of Lemonade (10/12)
They Hail the Chefs (10/16)
Superstars Shine for all the Heroes (10/21)
Restaurateur & Miss USA Feed Heroes (10/23)
Gift From the Heart of Upstate (11/19)
Artists to Help Sept. 11 Victims (11/26)

Heroes Emerge Amid Chaos (9/12)
Corporate Bigs Open Wallets (9/13)
Rescuers Flock to City – Samaritans From Nearby States (9/13)
Six Living Miracles Emerge From the Rubble (9/14)
Torrent of Thanks for Bravest (9/14)
Volunteers Are Lining Up by the Thousands (9/15)
WTC Love Story Has a Happy Ending (9/15)
N.Y. at Its Best Unites in Prayer (9/17)
B'Way Opens Its Heart (9/18)

9/11: Stories of Courage, Heroism and Generosity

Compiled by Tim Zagat

First Edition 2011 • Printed in the U.S.A.

Library of Congress Cataloging-in-Publication Data is available.

Typography and book design by Zagat Survey, LLC.

ISBN -13: 978-160478465-7

Published by Zagat Survey, LLC, 4 Columbus Circle, New York 10019

Dedicated to:

*Everyone who suffered a loss on 9/11
and everyone who helped out afterwards*

Table of Contents

Introduction

They were our husbands and wives, our mothers
and fathers, our brothers, cousins, neighbors, friends,
colleagues, lovers. Busboys and businessmen, pilots
and programmers, secretaries and socialites, firefighters
and financiers. They were heroes by choice, they were
heroes by chance. They were loved, and they were lost.
Portraits of Grief, The New York Times

Tim Zagat: It was Saturday, September 8. Nina
and I zoomed up 107 floors with Takao Sasakawa,
a Japanese businessman, and his bride, Junko, whom
we were shepherding around New York. As usual,
the elevator went up so fast that we were all a bit
dizzy when we stumbled out into the grand, full-floor
space of Windows on the World. Often referred to as
"WOW," that was the renowned restaurant on the
107th floor of the World Trade Center's North Tower.
Looking out from there was no less disorienting. We
could see 50 miles in every direction—Connecticut
out one set of windows, Queens, Brooklyn and Long
Island out another, and across Northern New Jersey
from a third. To see the Statue of Liberty, a mile away,
we had to press up against the south-facing window
and look almost straight down.

Any perspective from the World Trade towers could only be described as majestic. While they were under construction in the late 1960's, Nina and I were working on Wall Street. We would take any chance we could to pass by the base and gaze up at the two towers rising. They looked like they went on forever, an amazing show of grandeur and power.

In the years since it was built, we visited the Trade Center many times for business meetings, to shop and to eat. When giving tours of New York City, which we did frequently, Windows on the World, founded by our friend Joe Baum, was usually on the itinerary. On the evening Nina and I entertained our Japanese friends, it once again did not disappoint.

However, 60 hours later, all of this—the restaurant, the towers, the grandeur—would crumble in two unimaginable avalanches, one floor pancaking down on another, over and over again. The events of that Tuesday morning, and their terrifying consequences, changed us all: 78 Windows on the World employees served breakfast that morning to about 100 guests; everyone who was there died. The chef, Michael Lomonaco, survived because he had gone downstairs to have his glasses tightened. In all, 2,752 innocent people perished at the WTC that day, most of them civilians, including nationals of over 70 countries.

One block west of the WTC, the global headquarters of companies such as American Express and Merrill Lynch were devastated and Lower Manhattan took on the look of a silent, gauzy, dust-covered moonscape that would last for weeks.

Shocked as I was to see the television images of the two planes striking the towers, it was not until those gigantic symbols of American power collapsed that the full meaning of the tragedy sunk into my mind.

Born, raised and having lived most of my life in the city, like so many others I wanted to do what I could to help. Fortunately, as chairman of NYC & Company, the tourism and marketing organization for New York, I was in a position to be of assistance.

On the morning of September 12, Mayor Giuliani called a meeting of everybody from the city's key agencies, as well as corporate leaders who might shed light on the problems or help fix them. Cristyne Nicholas, my dynamic president, and I were invited.

The tasks were monumental: feeding thousands of workers at Ground Zero, searching for survivors, getting Wall Street's damaged communications systems up and running, reopening the Stock Exchange, finding accommodations for stranded travelers, attending to distraught families and on and on. But unlike what typically happens when people meet to talk about big projects, there was no discussion of lawyers, board approvals or even money. Everybody in that room said, "Oh, just tell us what needs to be done, and we'll do it."

Those words echoed throughout the city. The crew on the Time Warner Center construction site just north of my office marched downtown almost as soon as the news broke, and immediately set to work removing concrete and debris from "the pile" in the hopes of finding survivors. A quarter-million Americans rushed to the Red Cross right after the attacks to donate blood. Mayor Giuliani received $30 million in donations on the first day after he set up a fund for families of public service workers who had been killed, eventually raising $227 million. Federal, State and City officials, who usually battled with each other, now cooperated seamlessly.

There was a wonderful outburst of kindness and generosity—the likes of which I had never seen before or since. People were simply doing whatever they could.

What we learned from that terrible day is, in fact, a heartening truth: in a crisis, the overwhelming response of people is to do good. Whether it was the heroism of the police and firefighters rushing into the towers without regard for their own safety, or ordinary citizens across the country sending supplies to workers at Ground Zero, the first instinct was to help. Just like at other historic crises, for example, the Blitz in London, 9/11 called on people to do extraordinary things, and they responded. Critical times are often a prism through which we can see ourselves, and what we saw after 9/11 was the essential goodness of our fellow man and woman.

We want to salute that spirit in this book, which is a collection of remarkable examples of *courage, heroism and generosity*. There's the downtown high school principal who first saved her students and later started a school in Afghanistan in honor of her sister who perished in one of the towers. And there's the Verizon manager whose incredible efforts were instrumental in getting Wall Street back up and running. Governor Pataki and Mayor Giuliani tell of their experiences at a time that elevated both of their reputations, and some of the world's top chefs remember how they turned a sightseeing ship into a first-class canteen for the Ground Zero workers. In the following pages, a few of these heroes tell their stories in their own words.

Of course, these are just a small selection of the many stories of heroism and generosity from 9/11.

Inside the front and back covers, we've included contemporaneous newspaper headlines that further reflect Americans' response to 9/11.

Now 10 years after the attacks, we think that it's important to remember not only our lost friends and loved ones, but also the good residing in us all.

Tim Zagat

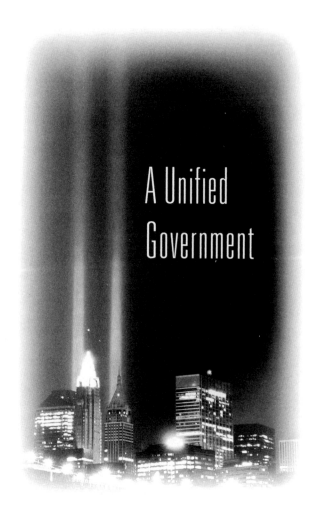

A Unified
Government

A Unified Government

Rudy Giuliani

George Pataki

On the morning of 9/11, Governor George Pataki and Mayor Rudy Giuliani found themselves at the center of the biggest crisis in New York's history. Both were near the close of long terms in office—Pataki 12 years, Giuliani eight. Though they had often been at odds, immediately after the 9/11 attacks the two leaders took the unprecedented step of merging their senior staffs to deal with the crisis as one government. In another unprecedented move, Pataki stepped aside to allow Giuliani to be the principal government spokesman, a role which the Mayor performed superbly. As a result, many people may not have realized that Pataki and Giuliani were working as a team. In this chapter, both describe how the spirit of cooperation they saw among everyday New Yorkers helped them and how 9/11 remains a moving lesson for turning a tragedy into something admirable.

George Pataki: Immediately after the attacks that morning my security team wanted to whisk me out of my Manhattan office.

"We're taking you to the heliport to go to the command center in Albany," a State Trooper said to me minutes after the first tower was hit.

It was the only time in 12 years that I refused a security direction.

"I'm going to stay in the city," I said.

I immediately contacted my chief counsel Jim McGuire and we began issuing the executive orders necessary to activate the National Guard and close the bridges, roads and subways to help secure the city. It was also primary day and we needed to take steps to suspend the election already underway.

With these measures underway I knew that if we were going to convince people to stay calm and optimistic in the face of terror and the unknown, I thought it was extraordinarily important that the government not go into hiding. That would be the worst thing we could do.

After talking to Mayor Giuliani and President Bush down in Florida, I felt it important to go downtown myself. Arriving at St. Vincent's Hospital right after the towers collapsed, I ran into Christy Ferer, the wife of Neil Levin, who I had appointed head of the Port Authority and a great friend. She was outside the hospital in tears.

"George, where's Neil? You have to find Neil for me," she said.

"Where was he?" I asked, trying to calm her down.

"He was having breakfast at Windows on the World."

I just said, "We'll try. We'll do our best." But I knew what the result was going to be.

The day was filled with many scenes like that, distraught people either fleeing the towers or looking for their missing loved ones. As I started to tally the toll this crisis was going to take, I saw a line of people a block long waiting outside the hospital. I assumed they, like many others, were looking to leave Lower Manhattan. But a fellow in line told me they were waiting to donate blood. "We want to help," he said. "We all do." I thought everyone would be trying to get off the island. Instead, they were waiting to give blood.

That was only one instance of the many inspiring ways New Yorkers responded to 9/11. From the first moments, ordinary citizens showed such strength that I knew we'd get through this. It didn't surprise me because I always had faith that America could meet any challenge. Still, some of the individual stories strike me as extraordinary:

There was Gene Flood, an ironworker, who, like so many men and women, dropped what he was doing to search for people in the wreckage. The morning of 9/11, he was running a crew working on one of the bridges between Manhattan and

Queens when they saw the towers come down. Realizing there was going to be a mess of twisted steel and metal, he knew he and his crew would be needed. Without any authorization, he commandeered his rig and his crew, taking them to Ground Zero, where they stayed every day until January 5.

Then there was Zack Zeng, a 28-year-old Chinese immigrant who came to the U.S. as a child and was working as a bank manager in Chinatown at the time of the attacks. Trained as an EMT, Zack was so proud to be an American that he felt compelled to rush to the scene. He turned his bank branch over to a colleague and cared for the injured at the WTC site. That's where he was when the towers came down. Zack died a hero, using his skills to help his fellow citizens.

That day, Americans were united; it was irrelevant whether we were young or old, black or white, Christian, Muslim or Jew, rich or poor. This was an unspeakable tragedy, but the sense of common purpose and humanity apparent in the first minutes gave me enormous confidence that we were going to get through this, and that we might even emerge a better, stronger, more unified country. It certainly unified New York's government.

When I was able to make contact with Rudy again around one o'clock, he told me he had set up a temporary command center at the Police Academy.

"I've got my team here," he said.

I took a two-second beat and then said, "All right. I'm coming with my team."

Out of all the decisions I had made that day (and there were a lot of them), this was by far the most important. What began that afternoon, with all the relevant members of both Rudy's cabinet and mine around a group of tables pushed together, became a unified command.

Moving our team to the Police Academy was absolutely critical for getting the City and State to work together seamlessly. Because we were together as decisions were made, we knew exactly who was responsible for what. It helped us make sure nothing was missed. We had to respond not only in the most coordinated and effective way possible, but we also needed the most positive, constructive public face for that response. Rudy was tremendous at the public aspect, and I didn't want competing voices or messages. So he became, appropriately, the public face of the response, while behind the scenes, both teams worked incredibly hard to make sure that everything that needed to be done was done.

It was very simple for me; in the wake of this tragedy, the idea of politicians fighting over camera time was just wrong. We owed it to the citizens, unified in their desire to do right, to do the same.

That Friday, the 14th, President George Bush, Rudy, Fire Commissioner Tom Van Essen, Police Commissioner Bernie

Kerik, Commissioner of Emergency Management Richie Sheirer and I were all packed into the President's limo driving up the West Side. We had just been at Ground Zero, where the President stood on the wreckage and told those working on the site that, "I hear you, and soon those who did this will hear us," to thunderous cheers of "USA, USA." Right from there, we headed to the Javits Center, all six of us mashed in and practically sitting on each other's laps. It was three days after the attacks, and the Ground Zero workers hoped that more people might be rescued. But you could feel that hope draining with each hour.

Now driving up the west side of Manhattan along the Hudson River, there were thousands of people cheering, waving the American flag and holding signs that read, "We love you, President Bush." It wasn't solely for the President; they had been there constantly, cheering every fire engine, every relief worker, every ambulance. It was an incredibly emotional sight.

Seeing this was incredibly heartening, since 9/11 was just a few days away and we had suffered an immense loss of life, infrastructure, safety and normalcy. There was a lot in jeopardy, including thousands of lives and the city's economic future.

But first we had to deal with the human catastrophe. I learned from the crash of TWA 800 in 1996, when there had been no provision for family members of the deceased. We had to set up an area where the loved ones of those missing could gather, get information and deal with their sudden, violent loss. I knew that this had to be a priority after the WTC attacks, because there were going to be thousands of family members going through the same unspeakable grief that I saw with TWA 800. So, on the afternoon of 9/11, we brought mental health and other counselors to the 24th Street Armory in Manhattan to help families cope.

The amount of need quickly overwhelmed our estimates and the Armory's confines. More and more people continued to show up with pictures of loved ones inscribed with the words, "Have you seen my son?" or "Have you seen my wife?" Soon we moved the family center over to Pier 94. Visiting the new facility, I was struck by the fact that many of the volunteers were people who had lost loved ones in other disasters. Reliving the tragedy of their lives they were able to help other people cope with the tragedy of 9/11. It was yet another example of the outpouring of inspiring humanity.

There was so much generosity that one of the serious problems we had was controlling the influx of volunteers. Because we had people coming from not just all over the country, but all over the world, we had to keep the situation from descending into chaos. I set up the Javits Center as a volunteer center where thousands upon thousands of volunteers were organized based on skill and need.

Puerto Rico sent up its terrific urban search and rescue team with dogs to hunt through the debris. Day two, when we still thought we could actually save lives, these guys were waiting in the Javits Center, chomping on the bit: "When will we get our turn? We're ready," they called. The next day they were sent down. Two weeks later, I ran into the Puerto Ricans down at Ground Zero. Transformed from their previously energized selves, they were utterly exhausted from sifting through the hot pile. Even their dogs were depleted, their pads worn down from the heat. People drove themselves into the ground helping, but they kept on working.

While dealing with the incredibly difficult human response, we also had to grapple with the enormous looming economic issues threatening not just the future of downtown, but also of the city. Almost immediately, there was a call to move in the opposite direction of the WTC and decentralize. *You can't have all the world financial giants concentrated in one neighborhood; you can't even have them in one city,* the critics argued. From day one, there was enormous pressure on companies to leave New York to avoid vulnerability—a potential nightmare. I asked my good friend and head of economic development Charles Gargano to immediately start up business recovery operations. So on the morning of September 12 we had converted the I Love NY call center to an emergency business hotline and established our economic emergency response team to help businesses find temporary relocation space, offer emergency financial assistance or anything else they needed. Within just a few days we had assisted literally thousands of displaced workers and businesses to get back to work.

Most important was Gargano's work to help reopen the NYSE and NASDAQ for trading. While the exchanges were not hit directly by the attack, the complex communications systems that facilitated trading were badly damaged. As the financial capital of the world and as the symbol of America's belief in free enterprise restoring trading was a national priority for our economy and our confidence.

The Friday after the attacks, I got a call from Ken Chenault, the head of American Express.

"Governor, we have a real problem here," he said. "I have a board meeting Monday. They want to leave Lower Manhattan. I don't want to go, but this is the second attack my people have been through. A lot of our workers are traumatized. I haven't been able to get anyone to provide me and our board assurance that if we stay here and go back into these buildings, we're going to have special security assistance that will allow us and our workers to feel safe where they are."

"Absolutely," I responded. "I guarantee you. Whatever it takes, we will make sure that happens."

If American Express left, then it would become virtually impossible to keep any of the other major institutions in Lower Manhattan. I knew that Ken's patriotism would beckon him to stay, but he needed to believe the promises of government officials that his workforce would be safe.

On Monday, the exchanges reopened trading and Ken called me, "The board met; we're staying in Lower Manhattan." With no written assurances, not even a handshake, he took my word and committed his great company to staying in Lower Manhattan.

Today, Ken is co-chair of the Partnership for New York City, the city's chamber of commerce. He was and is a patriot.

To this day, every time I go to the WTC site, I have a sense of tremendous sorrow at the loss of life that occurred there. And at the same time an equally strong sense of pride over the courage and strength that New Yorkers, and Americans from every walk of life, showed during that time.

When we started to contemplate creating a memorial and a master plan for rebuilding Ground Zero, I thought it was absolutely necessary to express both of these conflicting emotions. That's what made me support Daniel Libeskind's plan, which conveyed the sadness of the attacks *and* strength of our freedom. At its core, the plan preserved the footprints of the tower as a memorial around which we would rebuild economic confidence through impressive towers. I was sure the architect's plan would easily win over the other four submissions.

So I was shocked to wake up on the morning of the

Lower Manhattan Development Corporation decision on the master plan and see a front page article in *The New York Times* predicting that the group would choose Rafael Viñoly's plan. It was terrible news. In that plan, steel structures that looked like skeletons were to rise up from where the towers once stood. I had grave concerns about building on the footprints and about having steel skeletons coming out of Ground Zero.

I called Mike Bloomberg, the new Mayor, and asked him if he had seen the article.

"So what do you think?" I asked.

"Well, I don't know," he said. "What do you think?"

"I think it's very, very bad."

So Mike and I went to the LMDC board meeting to hear final thoughts before the vote. After questioning both Vinoly and Libeskind, I made a plea for the Libeskind plan to the board. But I'll never forget Mike's comment.

"The Viñoly towers look exactly like the fuel tanks I had to pay $30 million to tear down in Astoria," he said.

We succeeded in changing the decision, and they wound up choosing the Libeskind master site plan, which was the cornerstone for everything to come.

Now when you see the voids, where the footprints of the towers stood, you get this powerful sense of loss. In the same view, there is also this dramatic new transportation hub being created and, eventually soaring to new heights, the tallest building ever built in the United States, the Freedom Tower, to mark how we came through the attack.

Just as I do every single time I visit what was once Ground Zero, people will sense those two polar, powerful emotions of loss and pride when they come here, not just this year or next, but for all generations.

Rudy Giuliani: September 11 is a day that evokes many emotions, recollections, thoughts and concerns. It is also a day that triggered an enormous outpouring of support and assistance from people of all persuasions, backgrounds and beliefs, from around the world. I saw it; I lived it; and am humbled by the heartwarming, remarkable response that demonstrated the resilience of America.

September 11 was Primary Day, a semi-holiday for those of us in government. So I had planned for a relatively slow morning that included breakfast at Fives, the restaurant at The Peninsula hotel, with Bill Simon, a former Assistant U.S. Attorney who worked with me while I was United States Attorney. He wanted to talk about a possible run for Governor of California. But when Bill, my chief counsel and longtime aide, Denny Young, and I were finishing breakfast, Patti Varrone, a detective with the NYPD, who served on my police detail, interrupted us with news that an airplane had hit the World Trade Center. As Denny and I left, Bill said, "Good luck.

God bless you," and then hugged us. For Denny and me, this was business as usual; at least twice a month, I got called out to major emergencies such as a big fire, subway derailment or hostage situation. A plane crash was bad, but this is New York, and along with its greatness, serious incidents do occur.

As our car approached Canal Street, we saw a big flash of light, and within seconds we got a call from the police that a second plane had hit the towers. The situation was no longer business as usual. We had been attacked.

Despite the chaos outside, the mood in the car was calm and deliberate. With Patti in the front seat next to my driver, and Denny and me in the back, we tried to get through to the Governor and White House, but cell service was flooded and hardly working. Everybody was doing his or her job and reinforced each other.

We still hadn't reached the President or Governor when we stopped about three blocks from the South Tower. Getting out of our SUV, I was met by Deputy Mayor Joe Lhota and Police Commissioner Bernie Kerik right behind him.

"It's really, really bad, Mayor. It's really bad," Joe said, "People are throwing themselves out of the building."

That can't be right. Joe's overreacting. It's terrible, but that's not right – I thought.

I looked up and I saw debris coming down from the building, but people? The idea was so horrendous I told myself it couldn't be true.

We walked towards the Fire Department command post. That street-level location afforded a view of both towers, a perfect position for the Fire Department to see the whole fire.

Before we made any decisions on how to proceed, I wanted to see what was happening and get the facts for myself. So we marched down toward the World Trade Center, which is when I passed Father Mychal Judge, the Fire Department chaplain. He was also headed towards the towers but in a different direction. Before we parted ways, I put out my hand and shook his hand.

"Pray for us," I said.

"I always do," he replied.

Although the priest smiled, he looked very tense. And despite the many fires and deaths the priest had been through, I had never seen Father Judge look tense.

Then it happened. A man threw himself out of something like the 101st floor. Out of all the images during the day, that one remains with me the most. It's the one that flipped my entire feeling about what was happening. It was in that moment that truly I realized this was way beyond anything we had ever handled.

Moments later, I got to see Chief Peter Ganci, the Fire Department's highest-ranking uniformed officer and incident commander, running the show. He didn't mince words.

"My guys can only get people out who are below the fire," he said.

Carrying the weight of the situation, I returned to the Merrill Lynch office, which had been turned into a fully functioning communications center. There were cops at every desk. More members of my administration were there, too. Finally we got through to the White House; Karl Rove's deputy, Chris Henick, was on the line. There were rumors that the country had been attacked 12 times, everywhere from the Sears Tower to the Pentagon.

"Has the Pentagon been attacked?" I asked Chris.

"Confirmed," he answered.

Confirmed?

Chris is not a military guy—he's a political guy—but all of a sudden the number two political director in the White House was talking like a staff sergeant.

God Almighty; we really are in the middle of a battle.

"May I talk to the President?" I asked, not knowing the President was in Florida.

"You can't right now. We're evacuating the White House. But the Vice President will call you back as quickly as possible."

My mind was trying to process everything: the President being rushed out the White House, the Pentagon attacked, New

York attacked, people jumping out of buildings. The big question was: how many times were we going to be hit? We had no idea.

While my staff and I were discussing other possible terrorist targets, the Vice President called. I went into another office to pick up the phone.

"Mr. Mayor, Vice President Cheney will be on in a minute. Please hang on," a White House secretary said.

"Thank you."

I was waiting for the Vice President when all of a sudden, I heard a little click in the phone and the desk began shaking. I looked outside my office and people were going under their desks. I had no idea what was going on. Outside the window, a debris-filled wind moved through the streets like the cloud of some kind of nuclear attack.

I had virtually the whole of New York City's government leadership with me, and suddenly it occurred to me that it would be tough if they all got wiped out. I mean, there would be nobody to run this place.

I probably would have done the same thing if I had to do it all over again. I do not believe you can adequately assess an emergency unless you see it, because people, even professionals, are very bad at describing them. Some exaggerate; some understate; most people can't see all of it.

John Lindsay taught me that. After I was elected, he asked

me to lunch at the Century Club to talk over being mayor. "Get up off your backside and go there," he said. "I couldn't get them to fill potholes no matter what I did. So I made a big deal about my going to Prospect Park and gave out a detailed route four days in advance, and, what do you know, all the potholes got fixed along those streets." If there is an emergency, and the mayor goes, everybody behaves better, Mayor Lindsay said.

He was right; everybody knows how important it is, cooperates more, works harder and gets the job done faster when the boss is there. Whatever I lost, in terms of the risks I took, I gained in my ability to manage the emergency and make better decisions.

The spirit of cooperation was amazing. It started from the highest levels when Governor Pataki and I agreed on 9/11— that very day— to have a joint command center at the Police Academy on 23rd Street with all my people and all of his. Within a day, the federal agencies joined us and what emerged was two months of joint meetings every day. We ran the city and the state together, so that all of his commissioners sat at the same table with all of my commissioners. And every single decision we made, we made together.

We never pointed fingers for a mistake, because in an emergency that's deadly. The Governor and I knew instinctively that if we sat down in the same place with our staffs together, they'd know we were serious about them working together.

We took joint ownership of the good decisions—and the bad ones, like originally choosing the Armory on Lexington and 24th Street for the family center. It seemed perfectly correct when we opened it up, but a couple of days into it, it was clear we had made a mistake. What seemed a grand open space turned small and dark with the crowds of grieving family members. The head of the Red Cross told me it was so bad that it was going to lead to depression.

That had to be an exaggeration. But on the recommendation of my now wife, Judith, I went down to see it myself and immediately realized the head of the Red Cross was absolutely right. It looked like pictures of Ellis Island from the turn of the century. We had underestimated the scope of the problem. The Armory seemed too small for the numbers of people who needed help.

Reversing that decision would have been difficult if the Governor and I weren't working together. There could have been a lot of recriminations. Instead, working together, we reversed our decision, and picked Pier 94 on the Hudson River as the new center where families would have plenty of room and plenty of light.

I had supported Mario Cuomo in the gubernatorial race against George Pataki, and we had different points of friction. But I really got close to him working together after 9/11 and had great respect for him as a leader. Earlier, when I was diagnosed with prostate cancer and had to drop out of the race for U.S. Senate, he and his wife, Libby, invited me to visit them at their house, just to talk. I spent half a day with them and it became much more personal. He is a fine person.

Right after the attacks, I wasn't sure we could manage what was clearly the worst crisis to hit the city. But after two long days of some uncertainty, I came to realize that, working with the assembled team, we were doing it.

I wasn't sure exactly how many were dead, how we were going to clean up the World Trade Center site, if we'd be hit with another terrorist attack, when the Stock Exchange was going to be up and running again or if businesses were going to permanently leave New York. I wasn't even sure if I was communicating correctly to the public.

Because I knew how important my messages to people were, I solicited the advice of a lot of professionals, including a group of experts on trauma and grief.

"I don't know the balance," I said to them. "We're all very upset. We can talk endlessly about how upset we are. But how much of that should we convey? And how much should we convey a stiff upper lip?"

"Don't program it," they said. "We've been watching you, and so far it seems to be working. Just go with it. Just be yourself."

So I followed my gut, not just in talking, but with everything.

But it wasn't until September 13 that I finally trusted it.

It was the night before President Bush was scheduled to arrive in New York City to visit Ground Zero. Governor Pataki and I had encouraged the President to come, and he finally decided to do it—even though the Secret Service had understandable reservations about his coming to Manhattan, let alone Ground Zero.

I'd been working all day and into the night to make sure the President would be safe. After we finished around 10 o'clock, I returned to my office with Judith. There I began to doubt my decision.

My God. Is this the right thing to bring the President here, now? Maybe somebody's going to shoot him, or something's going to fall on him.

I suddenly felt a searing pain in my body.

"Judith, I've got shooting pains in my shoulder," I said. I started to think maybe I was having a heart attack.

A trained nurse, she asked me to show her where the pain was.

"You're not having a heart attack. It's stress. That's all," she said. "The meetings are over. Why don't you just go take a walk? Get yourself out of this atmosphere. You'll be able to think better."

Judith talked to a couple of my guys, who took me in one car rather than the usual two or three we were using at that point. I didn't want to go too far, so we ended up in the middle of Stuyvesant Town. The courtyard in the middle of this downtown housing complex was completely empty. Everybody was inside watching television.

"Give me some room," I told the two officers.

It was the first time I really had time to think since September 11. In that quiet space, I remembered I had banged my shoulder when someone pushed me into a car right after the attacks. I immediately relaxed after figuring out the source of the pain.

I kept walking east, out of Stuyvesant Town, and toward the East River. I passed a few shocked citizens, who must have thought the mayor had really gone nuts. I ended up at the East River. I was suddenly, and unexpectedly, completely reassured by the calming, constant natural flow of the water. I realized that a part of me wasn't sure it was going to be there. And it was there. That's when I knew everything would be okay.

Having been mayor of New York City for seven and a half years, I had probably overseen more emergencies than anyone else in the country. I loved running things. Still, in the past I had been accustomed to a certain amount of time to make a decision. I'd try to get my deputy mayors to debate me on why I might be wrong. A deliberative process was crucial for avoiding mistakes.

In a situation like this, there was no time. After 9/11, I would make three or four decisions, and then I would stop and say a prayer: "Dear God, make it right." At the river, I reconciled that I wasn't going to make all the right decisions, and I couldn't get angry at myself for not being perfect.

The psychiatrists had told me to communicate by instinct, be honest and do it from the heart. That gave me a sense of confidence. I was in charge as much as anyone could really be in charge. I turned from the river and returned to my office. And from then on, there wasn't any real indecision.

Almost immediately after the attacks, I wanted to encourage people to get back to normal, but everyone mourns differently. There were some who were ready to jump back into their routines right away, and others who weren't. I felt it was my job to create the atmosphere where if you were ready, then there was nothing wrong with that. And if you weren't, it was also okay to mourn a little longer.

But I knew the city needed a release. So the very next day, I started saying to the world, "You should come to Broadway. Go to a play. Come and spend money in New York. We need your money."

We did need the money. But we also needed to restore our morale. I remember how good it made me feel to see visitors arrive from all over the world. One delegation of 22,000 people from Canada arrived, and Times Square was filled with Canadians. It made me feel like we weren't alone, and I'm sure it made a lot of other people feel the same way. Just like when there's a death, friends and family gather for support during a funeral, wake or shiva, I wanted people to come and be a part of the city to support those of us who lived here. I used to say, "Come to New York as an act of defiance. Show the terrorists they didn't win."

I encouraged everyone to go back to work, including Major League Baseball and David Letterman, who made a big deal of it on his show. "The mayor told us it's okay to go on," he said. The second Saturday after 9/11, I opened *Saturday Night Live* with NYPD Commissioner Bernie Kerik, FDNY Commissioner Tom Von Essen, and a bunch of firefighters and police officers. The show's creator, Lorne Michaels, came up with a great bit. "Is it okay for us to be funny?" he asked. And my line was, "Why are you going to start now?"

It wasn't just me putting out the message. Some of New York's biggest names loaned their star power, and good humor, by participating in a series of ads that encouraged people to come to New York. They included people like Barbara Walters, Henry Kissinger and Woody Allen doing things like dancing like a ballerina, sliding into home plate or skating at Rockefeller Center. The ads were amazingly well done, especially considering they took about three days to complete.

Everyone contributed whatever he or she could. Construction workers were relentlessly assisting the overworked members of our different agencies—the Fire Department, Police Department, Sanitation Department and others—to clear debris from the collapsed World Trade Center with hopes of finding survivors. People, restaurants, and other companies and organizations were offering food and water to the workers, and so much more to those displaced from their homes or offices. About three weeks after 9/11, I was driving near 42nd Street when I noticed the cop directing traffic was wearing a hat covered in squares, the funny uniform of the Chicago police. I asked my driver to stop.

"Hey, what are you doing here?" I asked him.

"Mayor Daley sent 500 of us here to help out," he said. "The NYPD has me doing traffic duty, so that officers can be released to do other things."

"Well, that's great. I want to thank you, and I want you to thank Mayor Daley," I said. "But how the hell do you know where to send people?"

Let's just say, there may be people still driving around the Bronx who he sent there.

Whether it was attending a funeral or creating the family center, helping out made me feel relevant and kept me from feeling sorry for myself—mostly. The massive loss would enter my mind, but then I would say, "I'll have to wait until later to mourn the loss of Father Judge, Pete Ganci and many others."

The fact that so many others also helped out kept me going.

Even though I'm a diehard Yankee fan, New York Mets owner Fred Wilpon and manager Bobby Valentine have my utmost respect for what they did right after September 11. The day before the Mets were to play their first game after the attacks, the team asked for as many Fire, Police and Port Authority hats as we could send. I didn't know why they wanted the hats. Perhaps to sign them and raise money, I imagined, which was a nice gesture.

They wound up doing something much nicer. The next night, when the Mets took the field, instead of wearing their team baseball hats, they ran out in the hats we'd given them. I'm not sure they have any idea how much that affected the families of 9/11 and the people working at Ground Zero. In New York City, most police officers and firefighters are avid sports fans. When I would go to the wakes and the funerals, probably 70 percent had sports memorabilia on: a Ranger jersey, a Yankee hat, a Giants shirt. So, when the Mets wore the department hats, it lifted people's spirits by making them feel important.

Ironically, the Mets got criticized by Major League Baseball, which told the team to put its regular hats back on. In an act of defiance, when the Mets played their next game in Pittsburgh, Bobby Valentine had the Mets wear the department hats again.

It was exactly the New York spirit—nobody tells us what to do.

There are so many stories of incredible generosity. A very, very big one started with a call a day or two after 9/11 that I made to Jeff Immelt, the newly installed head of G.E., to see if he could expedite sending generators to Ground Zero. I knew his predecessor, the legendary Jack Welch, but I didn't know Jeff Immelt. As soon as I got him on the phone, he assured me we'd get the generators we needed right away. Then he said, "You know, my people have been talking and we would like to donate some money to help the firefighters and the police officers. They were very special in the way they handled this. Do you have such a fund in the city?"

"Yes, we have funds like that in the city," I said.

"Well, good. If you could just have somebody call back my office and give us the information, we'll send the check for $10 million."

Ten million?

Mike Hoffman, who runs the philanthropic company Changing Our World, and Larry Levy, one of the best lawyers you'll ever meet, sat down that very afternoon and developed the Twin Towers Fund. The next day, Rupert Murdoch pledged an equal amount and by the time Jeff Immelt announced the fund, we were already at something like $30 million. In three months, we raised $216 million, every penny of which we distributed within a year and a half.

A Unified Government: *Rudy Giuliani, George Pataki*

It wasn't just the Wall Street executives and financial big guys who made a difference. Far from it. People from all walks of life gave whatever they could in terms of time, money, resources and spirit to get New York back on its feet. The image that always chokes me up was that of hundreds of laborers streaming down the West Side Highway and into Ground Zero the afternoon of the attacks. As I watched iron workers, crane operators, carpenters and sanitation workers, who showed up without being asked, I knew this city was going to be okay.

Later that day, the firefighters planted the American flag on the pile. The moment, reminiscent of Iwo Jima, made me realize that Americans fight back. I had read Tom Brokaw's book *The Greatest Generation* over the summer, and the question that was left open was: Could this generation handle what that generation handled? And when I saw that flag being planted, I knew the answer was...yes!

Not too long ago, I began to think that people had forgotten 9/11, but after Osama bin Laden was killed, I realized they haven't. When I saw the celebrating in Washington and New York, my first reaction was unease. *Why are they celebrating? The war isn't over. This will be a bad signal and could be misunderstood by the Muslim people.* All of that is true. But on the other hand it showed that there is still an emotional connection to the attacks. Ask any American, and he or she can tell you where he or she was that day. No one has forgotten.

It's human nature that we have to be challenged for the best in us to come out. For our generation, 9/11 was the defining moment.

Continuing
the Fight

Continuing the Fight

Deborah Borza *Gordon Felt* *Patrick White*

When the 40 passengers and crew members aboard United Airlines Flight 93 crashed their plane in a field in rural Pennsylvania to avoid a greater tragedy, they instantly became national heroes. But seven years later, when a memorial dedicated to their courage was stalled by bureaucracy and greed, family members and friends stepped in to make sure everyone made good on their promises. Their determination would mirror the bravery and courage of the loved ones they were honoring.

Gordon Felt: My brother Ed lived in New Jersey with his wife and two daughters and had been traveling for work. He was employed by a company called BEA Systems, but none of us ever really understood what he did. He was some kind of troubleshooter for a system that encrypted financial transactions over the Internet. If something wasn't working, they'd send in Ed. He went all over the world to solve problems.

Ed was constantly curious, taking things apart and putting them back together. When he was six years old, my parents found him in the basement trying to rewire the electric circuit box in the house. Once he got his hooks into something, he relentlessly learned all he could about it.

I couldn't imagine that my brother was now scattered over a reclaimed strip mine in Pennsylvania. My anger rose even as I tried to push the details of the story out of my head: His plane had come down at about 600 miles an hour, traveling upside down as it just cleared the rooftop of a recycling business, and nosed into the ground at the bottom of the bowl of the filled-in mine. Missing a school by seconds, it disintegrated on impact, shaking the ground and blasting debris into the grove of hemlock trees ringing the site.

The local coroner, Wally Miller, immediately recognized that the whole area, including the crater where they would dig out the black box and small items from the passengers onboard, needed to be treated as a crime scene. The remains of our loved ones were ashes scattered across rocks, dirt, grass and wildflowers. Our murdered family members covered the land.

So it was closed off and protected as a crime scene for six days until the FBI had opened the crash site to family members—which is how I found myself on a bus to visit the scene for the first time.

I remained in my personal fog as the bus left for the site. The faces around me, the area's rolling hills, the small town road—they all were irrelevant. Then something finally caught my eye. I looked out the window and saw people at every intersection and on every lawn. There were police officers, troopers and firefighters standing in salute, and ordinary citizens and their children waving flags. For the 20-mile drive to the crash site, the entire road was lined with local people standing in solidarity with us and paying tribute to our grief.

I wanted to be left alone with my thoughts so I could mourn my brother. But the pain and compassion stretched across all those faces proved this loss was bigger than losing a brother or any of the other losses experienced by the passengers on the bus. History was unfolding in front of us.

Although the reality is that we will never really know exactly what happened on that plane, we know collective action took place and that all the passengers and flight crew lost their lives. We know that if they hadn't taken action, that plane could have crashed into the White House or the Capitol Building, or it might have been shot down. All of those options would have dealt a blow of far worse impact to our country.

That's what compelled the people of Shanksville to salute us in the buses, the first of many tributes to come. About a week later, President Bush and the First Lady, wanting to honor our loved ones, invited all of us to the White House. Getting to meet the President, who spent time with each family, was a privilege. Yet, the most startling part of the visit came when White House staffers lined the corridors and clapped as we exited the building. These were the folks who would have been whisked out into bunkers if Flight 93 had headed for the White House.

The brave and selfless action my brother and the others on the plane took was truly special. It gave us hope and something to hold onto in those dark hours. And as their family members, we had a special purpose to tell their story for them and for our country.

So one year after Flight 93 crashed, after many of us returned to Shanksville for the first memorial service, we held our first family-member meeting. In the past year, the National Park Service, realizing the significance of the land, began the process of turning it into a historic site. Some of the family members also realized that if we were to have a seat at the table, we needed a structure. So an organization was born.

When President Bush signed the Flight 93 National Memorial Act on September 24, 2002, it signaled our country's resolve in supporting our mission. An Act of Congress created a federal advisory commission to oversee the memorial and recognized a unique partnership among the federal government, the National Park Service, the state, the local community and family members to create a design, secure the land, raise the funds and finally build a memorial.

From day one, it has been a lot of work. It's nothing for me to put in 20 to 30 hours a week traveling, having phone meetings, receiving reports, giving reports, drumming up support or keeping our partners in the loop. I am overwhelmed with oceans of e-mail.

But everyone is dedicated to getting it done. Even the local community in Shanksville works tirelessly to maintain the memory of what happened there. This little rural community was transformed by an event that turned it into a national focal point.

Since the site was first opened to the public, thousands of people have visited the empty field surrounded by rolling hills. Wanting to connect to the day, these visitors started leaving behind tributes of their own. They placed notes, patches, boots, flags and more on the ground or under rocks. Donna Glessner, a Shanksville resident, realized that someone needed to care for this makeshift memorial and answer visitors' questions about what happened on 9/11. So she organized a group of about 50 volunteers, now known as "the ambassadors," who continue to be the chief stewards of the site.

From sunrise to sundown, 365 days a year, they stand outside or sit in their cars, keeping an eye on the land for us. More than 1.4 million visitors have been greeted by them. They are as much a part of the story as the families.

A host of emotions have fueled all of us who joined in the effort to get a national memorial built. There is gratitude to Donna and all the people like her who have generously offered to help. There's pride in the heroic deeds of our loved ones. But there is also anger. My brother was murdered— my brother who took up piano when his daughter started playing and read through *The Wall Street Journal* with his other daughter every single morning. The only motive behind his murder was terror.

I heard it myself when the families were brought together to listen to the voice cockpit recorder. We all went into that meeting hoping to hear our loved ones and get information that might lead us to a better understanding of what happened. But instead we heard the horrendous sounds of people dying who knew they were dying.

I owed it to my brother to not drown in that anger. The memorial gave me a way to channel it into passion for a cause. The passengers of Flight 93 chose their destiny. They could have sat by and let someone else dictate how their lives were going to end. But they chose not to. They chose to collectively discuss, talk and act. They voted.

That's why we bristle a bit when people categorize our loved ones as victims. We don't consider them victims at all because they fought back. They did what they thought they needed to do. And that is inspiring.

I tried to emulate that spirit in my work as president of the Families of Flight 93. If we wanted to get something done to pay homage to those 40 passengers and crew, we had to work together through the bureaucratic tangles, disagreements and roadblocks. What kept me going when I got tired or frustrated or just emotionally overwhelmed was one thought: Compared to what my brother Ed and those other people did, nothing is difficult.

Patrick White: We could have all the good intentions, big donations and political support in the world. But if we didn't have the dirt, we couldn't build a memorial.

Seven years after the crash, the Families of Flight 93 faced the somber fact that although we had a winning design, we still didn't have an agreement on the land to start the 2,200-acre park. Despite the Memorial Act Congress had unanimously passed and President Bush had signed into law, and despite the private money that had been raised and the government funds promised us, we ran into a dead end trying to buy the 273-acre tract that included most of the crash site.

In December of 2008, after two years of trying to fashion a way to acquire that property from the people who owned the stone and gravel mine, we were no further along than when we started.

I'm a land-use lawyer; this is what I do for a living. So no matter the awful circumstances that spurred this project, I set about it like I would any other. We had a source of funds that I could use to negotiate, including $600,000 from the folks in the community and other sources, and a donation from Universal Studios, which gave us the proceeds from the weekend opening of their film *United 93* that amounted to approximately $1.4 million.

I thought that would be more than enough to buy a field in the middle of rural Pennsylvania, especially since by then the families had already acquired two tracts of nearby land. But the stone and gravel company owners said although they were told their property was worth $50 million, they would settle for $10 million. I couldn't believe it.

We had a hard time getting them to commit to even a process to determine a fair sale price. We offered to pay for the land to be surveyed: Nope. We offered to pay for an appraisal: Nope. We offered to get a panel of appraiser arbitrators: Nope. Frustration turned to anger when I learned they were talking to a "stigma appraiser" from the West Coast. Those are the people who see how much a property like Nicole Brown Simpson's condo is worth after she was murdered there. They were trying to game the system, not negotiate in good faith.

The company owners canceled the lease twice for the land that held the temporary memorial containing the hundreds of objects visitors had left behind to pay tribute. When they threatened to cancel it a third time, we moved the makeshift memorial across the street to lands we had most recently acquired because we just couldn't be put in that position any longer.

There was a part of me that wanted to tell the property owners off and simply walk away from the whole thing. But when I thought about my cousin Joey Nacke, who died on the flight, there was no way in hell I could do that. He was never afraid of anything or anyone—including me. Even though I was seven years older and supposed to be the enforcer when we were kids, there was no backing down for the guy.

As an adult, Joey remained fearless. He had a Superman tattoo on his arm to commemorate the time when he badly injured himself as a little kid after flying through a plate glass sliding door wearing his Superman costume and cape. It never surprised me that he was one of the guys who stormed the cockpit. His remains were found a distance from the crash site, after the cockpit broke off from the rest of the plane. And his siblings later heard his voice on the cockpit voice recorder.

I couldn't let the rest of my family down either. All of the aunts and uncles on my mom's side are an integral part of the fabric of my family; the cousins I have are all younger than me and as close as my siblings. When we were first allowed to view the crash sites, 52 members of our clan took up the entire first bus. And the guy at the front of the bus was Joey's dad, my uncle Paul, whom we lost seven weeks later when he suffered a heart attack. People talk about dying from a broken heart and I understand that now.

I used my fury over his and the others' loss to attack the mountain of paperwork and mile-long list of phone calls that awaited me in trying to move the land deals for the memorial forward. If we didn't break ground by the summer of 2009 there was no way we were going to make our goal of having the first portion of the memorial built by the 10-year anniversary.

That's where the Families of Flight 93 drew a line in the sand. To hit 10 years and not have anything tangible to show the families and friends of those who had been killed would have been too painful. I had spent more than two years believing we could come to an agreement on the sacred ground parcels but not quite knowing what it would take. Now I knew. We had to get tough and do it immediately.

If the quarry company owners wouldn't sell their land in a voluntary way, then the government needed to step in and seize it. We had worked with the federal government to get the power to use the laws of eminent domain for the memorial, but we were coming down to the end of the Bush administration. Our best chance for action was from the President who had signed the Memorial Act. Who knew where we would land on the next President's list of priorities? So the Families of

Flight 93 wrote a letter to President Bush in November asking him to seize the land that held the remains of our loved ones.

Weeks passed and then a month, and we still hadn't received any kind of response from the White House. With every day that went by, the grim reality of facing all those family members with bad news became more real. As the pressure mounted, we had to find another way.

On Sunday, December 28, *The Washington Post* printed a front-page story highlighting the concerns of the families and our request for President Bush to take the land. If there was any kind of public opinion battle, we knew we would win it. And we had to win this land war quickly.

Almost immediately we got a signal from the White House that there had been contact between high-placed officials and the land owners. Still, it came down to the wire. It wasn't until 11 p.m. on January 19, the last night President Bush was in office, when I saw the last of the faxed copies of the signed agreement to transfer the land. As the machine spit out the paper and I actually had them in my hand, I felt a tremendous sense of satisfaction at having done my job—and then a great deal of humility for being trusted to make sure it happened.

As a lawyer I value such agreements, but that paper was nothing in comparison to seeing the "dirt" move in the ground-breaking ceremony. That was the first tangible moment of progress after seven years of sketches, designs, fund raising and finally purchasing the necessary land. Many people who had helped us succeed were on hand—such as Secretary of the Interior Ken Salazar and Pennsylvania Governor Ed Rendell—but it was children who took the shiny silver shovels and turned the earth. They symbolized our future and the reason we're building a memorial.

I found it is almost inescapably difficult at times to do all this. It required inscrutability and infinite patience, not qualities I'd say I possessed in abundance at the beginning of this process. As a result of the memorial effort, I am not only a better lawyer but also a better person.

Deborah Borza: I don't want people going to the memorial and just being sad. I don't want them only to remember how horrible that day was.

The final resting place of my daughter Deora and the 39 other passengers and crew aboard Flight 93 is certainly sacred ground. The architect of the memorial, Paul Murdoch, did a great job respecting both that fact and the natural beauty of the land. There are no plans to change that resting place; the crash site looks as it did on September 10, 2001, with its natural vegetation, a grove of hemlock trees in the background and the local wildlife of deer, geese, grasshoppers, butterflies and birds. It's going to stay as it was before the plane crashed at 10:03 a.m.

Otherwise the area is transformed. The entrance to the memorial is marked by the Tower of Voices, a tower holding

40 wind chimes. Forty granite stones, each bearing the name of a passenger or crew member, run down to the site, symbolically tracking the flight path of the plane.

When visitors look over the wall at the sacred space I want them to take away inspiration from the actions of the passengers and crew of Flight 93. Just like it says in our mission statement, this is a place to "reflect on the power of individuals who choose to make a difference."

Deora had caught Flight 93 as a standby to head back to Santa Clara University for the start of her junior year. Although she was only 20 when she died, her short life had a big impact. She was always volunteering. At college, she worked with kids through the America Reach program. She helped first and second graders at a local elementary school, whose reading room now bears her name. Deora was upbeat, positive and considerate of others. It's kind of ironic since her name means tears in Gaelic. But I didn't learn that until later.

It hasn't been easy. When all the family members go back to our private space, where no one is looking, we have our own emotional moments. In that moment, I feel the void. I can either fill my personal void with sorrow and hatred and all of that, or I can spend the rest of my life filling it by making a difference, honoring Deora in a way that fits.

I don't want Deora to be remembered as some girl who didn't live out her life but as a young woman whose life is carried on in others. People are helping me do that. The public is very giving.

There were four teenage boys who made a difference. Taking off from Toledo, Ohio, they were determined to walk all the way to Ground Zero to raise money. On their way, they stopped at Shanksville and donated some of the proceeds to the memorial.

There was a social worker named Greg who made a difference. He had met Deora at the Helen Woodward Animal Facility in San Diego where she volunteered with troubled youth who came to ride horses. When he learned about Deora dying, Greg began organizing rock music benefits for the memorial. He raised over $2,000 by getting bands to play at bars and donate the cover charge. I attended one concert and couldn't believe the band players with nose rings and tattoos would be willing to donate their time. I fell in love with them.

I see Deora in these people and I surround myself with them. It's not just those who have raised money, but parents who have reunited with children, friends who have decided to support a cause or anyone else inspired by the courage of the 40 on that plane to make a difference. These living examples comfort and reenergize me, and help me to see the difference I'm making.

Everyone's
Best
Friend

Everyone's Best Friend

Frank Shane & Nikie

Frank Shane broke every rule in the pet therapy handbook when he brought his Golden Retriever, Nikie, down to Ground Zero. There was no protocol for anything—from the kind of footwear Nikie should wear on the pile to how Frank should deal with the unfathomable grief of 9/11. Yet, from the moment Frank and his dog stepped onto the site, they both knew they had a job to do. As it turned out, a pair of soft ears and a wagging tail offered one of the best ways to connect to the people on the ground.

Frank Shane: A day after the attacks, Nikie and I were walking around the Family Assistance Center when a woman made a beeline for us.

Trained in crisis intervention, I had decided to bring Nikie to the Center at Pier 94, set up by the city to help families of 9/11's missing or dead, because I thought he might cheer up some of the kids whose parents were navigating this unbelievable tragedy.

The woman tackled Nikie and threw her arms around him.

"Hello," I said.

The woman didn't respond and she didn't let go.

"What's your name?" I tried again.

Nothing. Despite Nikie's and my many experiences working with people in hospitals and trauma centers, we had never elicited this kind of emotion before.

A mental health worker came over and began to talk to the woman about the dog. When she finally did speak, the woman said she had a dog named Ginger.

"My husband loved to throw a yellow ball to Ginger," she said.

Slowly the mental health worker elicited from the woman that she needed financial assistance because her husband, who was missing, was the breadwinner of the family and brought her over to the right place for that.

In that moment, I recognized the power of an animal in making a human connection. I had learned about the incredible ability of dogs—and in particular Nikie—to communicate while working with him in a New Jersey brain trauma center years before 9/11. Nikie, a majestic Golden Retriever, was smart and intuitive. But I didn't know just how smart until I saw him in action at the trauma center. Whenever we went into a comatose patient's room, Nikie had a special demeanor. But if a patient was more alert, he approached them for a scratch or some kind of contact. Often the connectivity between him and patients broke through obstacles that doctors and nurses couldn't overcome.

Once we went into a room with a young girl, whose eyes were open as she lay in bed surrounded by her family. As he was trained to do, Nikie went behind the bed so that he didn't step on any cords, and I asked permission from the family to be there. I looked over at the bulletin board where within seconds you could get an idea of the patient's entire life. Her name was Lil and it was apparent from pictures of her shower and a wedding invitation that she was going to get married.

Suddenly, Lil let out a bloodcurdling scream. I panicked: Nikie must have stepped on something. We needed to get out of there, gracefully and fast. I pulled at Nikie's collar, but was stopped.

"No, no. Don't leave," Lil's mother said. "She just called out the name of her dog."

The doctors had never expected Lil to talk again.

From then on, every Sunday, Nikie made a point of finding Lil. Her eyes always had the vacant stare of patients with brain damage but she seemed to be more relaxed when the dog was there. We witnessed her improvement to the point of sitting in a wheelchair and seeming to blink in response to Nikie. Then one day, we arrived at the center and Nikie refused to get out of the elevator.

"Come on Nikie," I said, but he wouldn't budge.

You don't want to bring the dog in if there is something wrong, so I brought him back to the jeep and went upstairs alone. When I checked in with the head nurse, she said, "I have some good news for you. Lil went home."

The unspoken bond animals can make with people is real, and I knew it could be helpful to those suffering after 9/11. Clearly this was not pet therapy at the pier. It was not a nursing home. You were dealing with the raw nerves of a tragedy on a scale that no one had ever seen before. Nikie and I could be the bridge between the scared, confused or shut down and the resources that could help make them better.

While the mental health worker accompanied the woman, who had been clutching Nikie for dear life, to the relevant area, Nikie and I escorted her kid to the Child Life Center. There, children were playing games, eating snacks and talking to counselors. One of the counselors asked if Nikie and I could stay for a bit since they really had their hands full. There was one child the counselor pointed to in the corner, a six-year-old girl who wouldn't talk. This was Nikie's specialty. We went over to her. First she petted Nikie. Then she began to ask questions.

Is he a boy?

Why are his ears so soft?

I asked her if she would like to play checkers with Nikie, and her eyes widened. I took Nikie's paw and moved the checkers, but I said he didn't know how to play the game. She dutifully explained the rules to Nikie, and, little by little, she started talking about her dog and then about her father.

Days later, I drove my jeep down Broadway, through armed police and military checkpoints, with Nikie beside me in the passenger seat. This was a defining day because we were going to Ground Zero. We had the credentials but no idea if this was going to work. I had no protocol, no script.

As we headed south and the streets became deserted except for debris, the scene turned surreal, like we were in a movie. Manhattan looked like a war zone. I stopped the jeep near the Marriott Marquis because Church Street was obliterated. A Humvee with military guys holding M-16s blocked the beginning of the street. I asked them where I could park, and they looked at me like I was from a different planet.

"Anywhere you want."

I looked at Nikie. As his handler, I had to be the leader of the pack, unafraid and in charge. This was obedience 101. If I got scared, I would transmit it directly to him. But I couldn't mask my emotions; downtown New York was destroyed. So here we were, a guy and his dog, scared.

I knelt down and put Nikie's boots over his paws. Typically, he hates putting them on, but for the first time he didn't fuss at all. That's when I paused and looked at him.

What the hell am I doing?

Am I here just so I can say I was at Ground Zero?

We hadn't gone more than a few feet when a firefighter approached us, got down on one knee and held Nikie. He wasn't holding the dog as tightly as the woman at the Family Assistance Center, but there was something very powerful going on. From that moment on, I didn't have any doubt that we had important work to do at Ground Zero, even if I wasn't sure what it would be.

Finally, the firefighter stood up and told me that my dog had the same color hair as his best friend and brother who had died in the attacks. The three of us started walking down Church Street, past the rest tent, talking the whole way. I didn't know anything about firefighter culture. I didn't realize "brother" is lingo for a fellow firefighter. And I didn't understand how much emotion they had. Like a lot of other people, I just saw a uniform. When we were about to part, he turned to us and said, "When will Nikie be on again?" I replied that we didn't have a schedule.

"I would like to see him again," he said. "Could you bring him over tomorrow night?"

I spent eight months at Ground Zero. Every day, Nikie and

I were learning, adapting, and then learning and adapting some more.

I saw firsthand the tremendous toll the rescue and recovery effort took on EMTs, iron workers, crane operators, firefighters and anyone else sifting through the debris. I didn't approach them unless they were taking a break (I didn't want to expose workers to warm and fuzzy when they needed to have their adrenaline up so they could do their job). Because the sense of urgency was so great, people didn't stay in the rest areas for long. So I had to work quickly. With the lights on all the time and constant noise, day and night did not exist.

When they found remains, everything and everyone stopped. Once, when the remains of a firefighter were discovered, we stayed at the bottom of the pit after the body had gone up with bagpipes in tow. A firefighter leaned over Nikie, and he didn't need to say a word. We walked with him to the top while a wind vortex blew papers around so it looked like it was snowing.

In the brain trauma center, Nikie was the live teddy bear that drew people over to me. Then it was my responsibility to see if someone needed help and if I could steer the person in that direction.

On the most superficial level, a guy with his dog offered a small break from the intensity. Folks would start talking to me after greeting Nikie, and I had to be a well-educated listener. Sometimes the hardest thing to do is let victims tell their story—you want to interject and console them. Instead I assessed: Some needed to know it was okay to take breaks, others needed more structured help and a referral. There were ways to solve problems and prevent them.

Credentialed with his picture, Nikie was a worker with full access to even restricted areas. We could go anywhere on that 16-acre site. I wasn't there for fame or glory or to take chances. I had a job to do. And Nikie gave me the ability to do that job.

Although we became a part of the culture of Ground Zero, I didn't let us become Ground Zero. I maintained a separation by spending time off, site and debriefing myself with counselors. We broke up our work week with one day at the piers so we weren't on the pile every day. I couldn't afford to be reckless and let myself get immersed.

Within a few weeks, I put together a veterinary protocol for Nikie that included putting talcum powder in his boots and weighing him every day. We would work eight-hour shifts on the site, but he always had his rest time. People became very protective of him. Soon I didn't have to carry a collapsible bowl for Nikie to drink or eat. I always knew there was food for him wherever we went. We would take naps on the pews of St. Paul's church. With his head on my stomach, he'd be snoring away.

Not everyone was able to maintain this kind of balance.

In fact most didn't. A lot of Ground Zero workers lost contact with their families as they started to form a new family, the Ground Zero family. That wasn't all bad, but when they would go home, family members would ask a million questions and they didn't want to talk about it. There was one guy, who got really burnt out working in the morgue and was told to take a week off. "I can't wait to get home," he said. "I am going to take my son fishing." Two days later he was back. When his wife asked him to take the trash out, the black plastic bags connected him with the human remains put into black plastic bags.

"I have to be here and be with people who understand," he told me.

The fabric of Ground Zero was made up of people from all walks of life, all colors, all religions, all jobs. You never heard anyone complain. There was a perfect bond of brotherhood that could never be replicated.

That's why the hardest day for all of us was May 28, 2002, when we were set to leave the site. Despite the unbelievable achievement of this group—that they had cleaned up the site in much less time and for less money than thought possible—a family was literally coming apart. After the last steel beam was cut, workers would march up the ramp to West Street, and that would be that. As much as this was a place of destruction, it was difficult to imagine leaving it behind. One worker, picking up a few stones, said "I want to take something tangible home."

That gave me an idea. A couple of days before the last beam was to be cut, I went over to Apollo Flag, a store in New Jersey, where I would buy Nikie's trademark flag scarves that he wore around his neck. We had gone through close to 100 scarves since I gave them away as a token of people's bond with Nikie. I asked a big guy named Frank, who was one of the owners, if he knew where I could get my hands on about 2,000 flags.

I told him about Nikie and me, our work at Ground Zero and the closing ceremonies. I wanted to get flags for all the workers, but I didn't have money to pay for them.

"Don't worry about that," he said. "Just tell me how many flags you need."

We had an expression on-site: "the force of Ground Zero." When things were meant to be, they happened. Even the most impossible thing would fall into place. There was a force there. There had to be some spiritual sanctity to a place that held the remains of thousands of people.

While looking for someone who knew how to fold a flag military-style, I discovered the commander of the Iwo Jima, in New York for Fleet Week, taking a tour of Ground Zero. He offered to have the sailors on his boat fold and return the flags for the ceremony. When I asked if the Navy could hand them out, however, the commander wasn't sure.

The young men and women of the Iwo Jima and other boats docked in New York, not only folded the flags but did one better. With no command or director order, these sailors walked from the upper piers around the Intrepid to Ground Zero and joined the firefighters and police officers, who paid tribute to the workers, by flanking the 10-story ramp that led down to the site during the ceremony. When the first worker's shoe hit the ramp after the beam came down, everyone on the ramp turned and saluted. It was beautiful. At the bottom of the ramp, Mayor Bloomberg handed each worker a flag.

The American flag weaved itself through the entire Ground Zero experience. There were the flags draped over gurneys containing found remains, and the enormous flag that hung from the scaffolding on one of the adjacent buildings. The flag represents the spirit of our country, and so did the men and women who cleaned up that site in eight months. It also had significance to Nikie, who offered his flag scarves as easily as he did his affection and compassion. Things happened through him. Just like we received the donated flags for the workers to take home from the place where we bought his scarves, so did many people get greater help through first bonding with Nikie. But he didn't need any credit, and I certainly wasn't going to take it either. I was just the guy with the dog.

Putting
Wall Street
Back Online

Putting Wall Street Back Online

Carl Russo

For most of his career, Carl Russo lived a quiet life. A native of Queens, he worked for Verizon and lived in a suburb of Long Island, where he and his wife raised four kids. Over 30 years at Verizon, he had worked himself up through the ranks. On September 11, 2001, he was the man responsible for the network that served the country's biggest banks and brokerage houses. His actions that day and in the days and weeks that followed transformed Russo and his co-workers into heroes, placing them next to firefighters and police officers in a lavish awards ceremony at the New York Stock Exchange.

Carl Russo: That Tuesday morning, I was at my desk by the usual time, 7:30 a.m., doing my normal routine—assessing the workload. Circuits needed checking. Changes needed to be made. Priority lists were quickly made and assignments dispatched.

There was no such thing as downtime with my job. I jokingly called my house in Long Island my "weekend house" because I really only saw it—and my wife Rosemarie and four kids—on the weekends. It wasn't unusual for me to get paged by the office when I was finally on a train headed home. Often the news had me turning around and catching the next train back into work.

From my windowless office, I managed the Enterprise Control Center—a system that linked all the important banks together. Everybody was mapped to everyone else. A broker at one firm could talk to someone at another by picking up a line. These were automatic ring-down lines for speed and ease. All 10,000 phones were interconnected in an intricate and fully engineered web.

I was focused, powering through my morning, when a colleague interrupted me with a call.

"Go look at the World Trade Center," he said.

"What?"

"Go look at the World Trade Center!"

Verizon's building on Pearl Street, right next to where the NYPD had its headquarters, had only a handful of windows. But each one faced the World Trade Center, with a beautiful view of the west side of Lower Manhattan.

I went outside to take a look and saw the first tower

burning. "Jeez, what happened?" I asked no one in particular. I figured there was some kind of explosion. The papers and other stuff floating down from the destroyed offices brought me back to my own work.

All right. An explosion. Ascertain what's up, what's down. Isolate, route around and fix it.

Then the second tower was hit. People started panicking. Some were crying, others screaming. There was talk that we were next, our building, a big shining target on the water's edge near the Brooklyn Bridge.

I turned away from the windows and started making action plans.

Disconnect these circuits. Route circuits around the buildings. Fix it.

As my people began tackling the tasks at hand, I went back out toward the windows to see what was going on. Soon after, the towers started collapsing, pancaking. There were no words to describe it. A tremendous dust cloud bloomed up and quickly shifted into a gigantic gray monster snaking its way the 15 blocks toward our building. From the 14th floor where I stood, I watched it wind through the streets, chasing terrified people, some of whom fell as they attempted to outrun it. On the Brooklyn Bridge, the lanes were jammed with cars as people desperately tried to flee the island. But the cloud crept toward them, too. Now it was approaching me.

After serving with the Marines, I applied for a job at the then New York Telephone Company because my sister-in-law said they were hiring. I started out in 1970 as a switching technician.

I worked hard. Still, when I was promoted to the major customer service center in the late '90s, I couldn't believe my luck. On my first day in my new job, I was in charge of service for some of our biggest customers, including the biggest banks, insurance companies and other financial institutions. As the years went by, these turned out to be some of the most demanding customers our company had, and because they utilized so many services, and impacted so many consumers and other businesses, you couldn't let them down.

If a circuit went down, within 10 minutes I would have inquiries from inside the company and from our customer asking, "When will this be fixed?"

These expectations were put to the ultimate test in the hours after the Trade Center attacks. I briefed my supervisor, who was in a different state, early in the evening of September 11.

"We're not so bad," I said over a conference call. Except for the circuits destroyed in the towers themselves, we were still functioning. The digital representation of our network—a picture on computer screens with icons for each building and all the circuits it holds—was entirely green except for the Trade Center towers. They both had gone red.

I was on stunned autopilot. So were the rest of the people working for me. Silence ruled the floor where employees monitored the network and responded to customers calling in. On occasion, people would start crying. Then they'd go back to work—I did the same thing. Those of us working for the Enterprise Network knew it was vital to keep Wall Street operational. We were charged with the business of this country.

On the conference call, I didn't get a response to my report that for the most part the Verizon network was up and running. Had I been too blunt when I said we weren't "so bad"? Then I realized the call had gone dead.

7 World Trade Center had fallen. I had last seen it burning, its red flames competing with an unusually vibrant sunset that evening. As a result of that collapse, some 300,000 telephone lines and 3.6 million high-capacity data circuits went out.

The network that connected Wall Street had major pieces of equipment in 140 West as well—five servers that contained all the intelligence responsible for mapping every single line we had. Tens of thousands of connections from brokers to vice presidents were searing in a massive fire.

I rushed back to the floor, and yelled out, "What does our network look like?"

None of my technicians needed to respond. On the monitors, all the icons representing the buildings we covered were red. I clicked on a building to find a floor—red—clicked again to a specific phone—red. Tens of thousands of red lights. Everything was gone.

Make an action plan. Get the basic network back. Fix it.

I assembled my information technology team. These guys were the best. We realized we were going to have to replace the servers.

"How are we going to get them?" I asked.

"We have to go directly to the manufacturer."

"Where are they?"

"Canada."

Terrific. It was already late at night, and all the borders were closed due to the attack that morning. I knew I'd get a call tomorrow morning asking when we'd be up and running. And attempting to retrieve our old servers from 140 West wasn't an option. So Canada it was.

Working the phones, we reached a local salesperson from the company at home, who got to his people in Canada. They went into the office and found the servers we needed, but they didn't know how they could get them over the border that night. Nobody could cross anymore and all flights were canceled. So I began calling government officials—I don't know who I called or how I even got their numbers, but I tracked them down. We got an exemption for our truck. State troopers would be waiting on the U.S. side to escort our haul directly to us.

Because the lines were miles and miles long at the Canadian border with Americans desperately trying to get back in, the Royal Canadian Mounted Police drove the truck to the front of the line where it was met by the state police.

We didn't get too much time to celebrate our success in attaining those servers. Soon, I was back on a conference call. Verizon had set up a bridge from the unaffected switching systems uptown. Most of the Wall Street firms were on the phone. Vice presidents and senior vice presidents were on, as well as Richard Grasso, the chairman of the New York Stock Exchange. I was in the spotlight.

"Well, Carl what's going on?" a senior VP from a brokerage house asked.

"We've got a lot of damage that we're still ascertaining."

"It's been 24 hours and we still don't have service?" a VP asked.

I still don't know who was on that phone call. All I knew was that Wall Street was panicked, I hadn't slept in more than 24 hours and these guys were not happy.

"Carl, when do you think we're going to be back up on the air?" someone else asked.

"It will take me two weeks."

I just threw that out there. I really had no idea what it was going to take.

"Oh, no, no, no. We can't wait two weeks. This is the U.S. economy we're talking about."

I explained to the group what the problem was:

"All the servers that have the intelligence, that says, 'this bank is mapped to that bank, who's mapped to another firm, who's mapped to someplace else,' it's all in our damaged West Street building," I explained.

As I said, excuses were not an option. We needed to get back up and fast. The technicians and I huddled again. It would take weeks for technicians sitting at the keyboard to map out all the connections on the new servers, and from the conference call I knew we didn't have that much time.

"We've got to get to the old servers," one of my IT employees said.

I looked at these tired guys. I'm not sure any of them had slept either. How were they going to crawl up 21 floors in a damaged building in complete darkness and carry those five pizza-box-sized servers back down? I shook my head. We didn't even know what condition the servers were in.

There was no other option, though. Three of my guys, Jay, Scott and James volunteered for the job. They received hazmat training and, on September 13, found themselves wearing heavy hot suits for protection as they climbed the 21 flights with nothing but flashlights to guide the way. I would have much preferred to send up people who did this kind of thing for a living, but we needed people who knew what they were pulling out and how to disconnect servers without doing more damage. All I could do was pray for their safety, which I did over and over again.

When they returned, sweaty messes and slightly dehydrated but triumphantly holding the servers, I felt we already succeeded. The fact that some of the intelligence was still usable was a bonus. If anything had happened to any of those guys, I don't know what I would have done.

Later that day, I got a call from headquarters.

"This is the plan. Monday morning will be the opening bell."

"To bring everybody up?" I asked.

"Yup."

"Okay. Now the race begins."

By Sunday night, it didn't seem like anyone was breathing. I sure wasn't.

"Tomorrow's opening bell. How we doing?" I asked.

I knew the answer. The screens said it all.

"We aren't doing," my guys working in the back room with the servers said. "Everything's still red."

No one was going to sleep that night. But we were accustomed to that. An eight-person crew worked 20-hour days. I hadn't left the office since I arrived at 7:30 a.m. on September 11. We took catnaps every now and then on a couch that happened to be nearby and washed up in the bathroom sink.

Our entire focus was on one thing—getting the network up for the Monday bell. Everybody knew what was at stake. If Wall Street didn't open Monday, it would jeopardize all the trades from the previous week and threaten New York's position as the financial capital of the world. I barked out orders day and night.

This is where it's going to fit downstream.

Look at that circuit connection again.

Who's responsible for that?

Somebody would always respond with the answer, but I had no idea who that *somebody* was because I didn't look up at the person talking.

And yet we still hadn't found *the* answer. Those damned red screens refused to change. We kept trying and trying. Meanwhile, I was doing whatever I could to provide my IT guys with the tools they needed for their work. I woke one man up in the wee hours of the morning to order 10,000 feet of cable for rewiring because one of my technicians needed it immediately.

We tried to reassemble the network in the back office using the information from the old servers and the hardware from the new servers, which had since arrived from Canada. Everybody who could do something did something. Even the non-technical people did whatever they could do—sweep the floor, get rid of garbage. I saw the best in each employee. And yet, the screens were still red.

The sun was now coming up.

"How we doing?" I asked again, hoping against hope.

They were going to reboot, try again, do this, do that.

I went back in my office and crumpled in my chair. There was no sense in riding my guys. I knew they were trying as hard as they could to solve whatever small kink lay hidden in the system. All I could do was wait and pray.

When the phone rang about 45 minutes before the opening bell with a friend from the company checking in on me, I said with all certainty, "We ain't gonna open. I made this commitment . . . and it ain't working."

A half hour before the opening bell, I was out on the floor pacing among the technicians sitting behind their PCs, the monitors still filled with that terrible red. There was nothing left to say. I just stared into space.

You can't rush anything. If you rush it, you might screw things up worse than they are.

All of a sudden I saw *dink, dink, dink, dink, dink*: A sea of green washed over the monitors. A half hour before opening bell, the network came alive. It was as if God kissed me.

As a cumulative *aaahhh* spread through the room, the tunnel vision that had kept me focused for the past week left. For the first time, I saw around me the tired but happy faces of all the people working to make this happen. They started to yell and shout, "Yes! Yes!" while I made my way back to my office.

Once inside, I fell to my knees and bowed my head.

Thank you, Jesus. Thank you. It's over.

I lifted my head up and saw my employees going back to work on the floor, doing what they do every day. I sat there for a few minutes more before I got on with it, too.

We got our big thank you several months later when Dick Grasso held a congratulatory lunch at the New York Stock Exchange's dining room for all the different groups involved with the rescue and rebuilding efforts downtown. Emergency services were there, as was the military. Verizon also had a table. The Enterprise Network was just one part of Verizon's restoration efforts after 9/11.

In five days, Verizon essentially rebuilt a temporary telecom system for Lower Manhattan. For the Stock Exchange alone, we created 1.5 million new circuits. About 3,000 employees worked 13- to 16-hour shifts to put in 14,000 new lines in streets that were closed or collapsed. A field force descended on the area, cutting out the damaged lines, splicing in new cables and covering them with rubber. The company estimated it was about six months of work compressed into less than a week and more work would be needed in the future.

As Grasso spoke at the luncheon, I stared in awe at the dining room, truly an ornate setting. I had never been there before, and it was one of the most gorgeous spots I had ever seen. There's a vase there that's about six-feet tall, which Catherine the Great sent over from Russia after the Stock Exchange lent her a bunch of money that she never repaid.

After the speech, each of us was awarded a medal that read, "Let freedom ring. We will never forget."

A couple of people from work pressed me to take a picture with Grasso, so I stood in the receiving line of the crowded dining room until we stood face to face.

"I'm Carl Russo."

"Thank you, Paul," he said.

I didn't need Grasso to know my name to feel that putting Wall Street back in business after 9/11 was the biggest accomplishment of my life. I didn't save anyone's life, but I did something good. It's tucked away in my mind in case I'm ever called to do something like that again. I know I can bring that person back out and contribute to this country—as well as the company.

This is my 41st year with Verizon. I've been around so long that if you cut my veins, I bleed the red and black colors of my company. They pay me a good salary, and I give them good work. I keep customers connected, in service and happy; that's what I do.

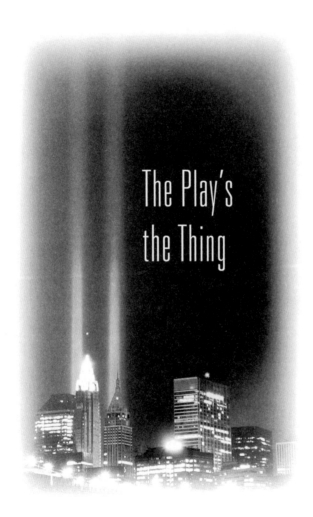

The Play's
the Thing

The Play's the Thing

Cristyne Nicholas

The attacks on 9/11 threatened New York's economy, not just by closing the Stock Exchange and downtown financial institutions, but also by spreading into the city's cultural life, restaurants, retailers and theaters. For a while, those industries' revenues were down 30% to 50%. It was quickly recognized that these businesses, at the heart and soul of the city's life, needed immediate help. They got it from the city's tourism and marketing organization, NYC & Company.

Cristyne Nicholas: The day after 9/11, Mayor Giuliani held a meeting at the police academy that reminded me of the 8 a.m. meetings we used to have daily when I worked for city hall. Sitting around a large table, members of his cabinet had to go around and brief the Mayor. On September 12, it wasn't only members of his cabinet but also other people important to the city like Dick Grasso, chairman of the

New York Stock Exchange, Joe Spinnato, president of the Hotel Association, Victor Ganzi, CEO of Hearst, Bill Rudin, head of the Association for a Better New York, Jed Bernstein, president of the League of American Theaters and Producers, Howard Rubenstein, New York's premier public relations man, and Jerry Speyer, chairman and CEO of Tishman Speyer, among many others. As president of NYC & Company, the city's tourism and marketing organization, I was also at the table.

"Cristyne, how quickly can the Broadway theaters get back and running?" the Mayor asked me. "How about tomorrow?"

I thought that was impossible, but I didn't say it.

"I'm concerned we won't be able to get the actors, who live in New Jersey and other places, into the city," I said.

"Make it their business to get in," said the Mayor, who understood that Broadway was at the heart and soul of the city. Thus, this was one of the first things my team tackled.

We worked out the logistics, including convincing some distraught actors to perform, and the shows went on, the very next night. I attended *The Full Monty*, where the house wasn't filled by any stretch of the imagination. At the end of the show, everyone in the audience and on stage broke out into a heartfelt rendition of "God Bless America." I later learned that theaters throughout the city had erupted into the same spontaneous show of patriotism. To support Broadway and tourism in general, with the investment of $2.5 million from the city's

Economic Development Agency, we purchased 50,000 tickets and simultaneously developed a promotion called "Spend Your Regards to Broadway" whereby anyone who spent $500 in a city museum, store or restaurant received a pair of tickets to a show. Pretty soon, the theaters were full again and shopping had become an act of patriotism.

After the attacks, those of us at NYC & Company were meeting around the clock with members from all aspects of the city's life. Our chairman, Tim Zagat, moved into our offices full time, Jon Tisch headed up a crisis committee called "New York City Rising" and our executive committee met once a week instead of quarterly. Everyone just wanted to help. First the attention was on Ground Zero. The hotels offered to house the rescue workers and families trying to find loved ones. The hoteliers made 25,000 hotel rooms available for office workers displaced by the attacks. The restaurants wanted to serve, too and provided an untold number of meals without charge.

Soon it became clear that the rescue workers weren't the only ones who needed help. In the following weeks, our focus shifted to trying to save the economy. We wanted to make sure that tourism—one of the top employers with 300,000 New Yorkers working in the industry at the time—didn't take more of a hit than it already had. Hotel occupancy was dramatically down, and the restaurant and retail businesses were off by as much as 50%. How could we help?

One of the first things we did was create an advertising campaign with the mayor's office, featuring celebrities having fantasy New York moments. In one, Barbara Walters was trying out for *Cats*. Woody Allen did triple toe Lutz loops at Rockefeller Center, and Henry Kissinger hit a home run and ran the bases at Yankee Stadium. These pro bono spots, which were produced by BBDO, ran for free all over the country. We worked with the late great Phil Dusenberry, longtime chairman of BBDO, along with his team led by John Osborn, Ted Sann, Michael Patti and Gerry Graf. They showed that New York was still a vibrant place—and that it was okay to laugh. If we New Yorkers could have a sense of humor in our darkest days, then anyone could.

To help the restaurant industry, we held a series of Restaurant Week promotions, starting in mid-October. Almost immediately, restaurant revenues returned to normal. Only Downtown continued to suffer. Two new promotions, "Christmas in Little Italy" and "Celebrate Chinese New Year," redressed that problem.

It was our job to put New York's best face out to the rest of the country. That's why we made sure all the city's most telegenic events went on as scheduled—from baseball to Fashion Week to the NYC Marathon to the Macy's Thanksgiving Day Parade. Mayor Michael Bloomberg was sworn in by Mayor Giuliani on New Year's Eve, just three months after the attacks, in Times Square right before the stroke of midnight. Over 600 million people from around the world watched.

Still, people were asking, "What can I do?" Once the blood banks were filled and the necessary trained rescue workers were in place, Americans didn't know how to show their support. So we came up with the idea of "patriotic tourism." Allow us to say thank you in person, we told the rest of America and eventually the world. We secured funds from New York State to invest in a $5 million campaign called "Paint the Town Red, White and Blue," where stars like Whoopi Goldberg, Regis Philbin, Kelly Ripa, Derek Jeter, Ben Stiller and others encouraged people to visit us.

We became cheerleaders for the city. Somebody had to boost the spirit of New Yorkers. It wasn't always easy, however. Like so many New Yorkers, I lost important people in my life like Father Mychal Judge, who had officiated at my wedding. A press conference to announce free flights to New York felt a little trivial when followed by such a friend's wake. But at NYC & Company, we felt like Atlas with the city on our shoulders and we couldn't let it down.

It was an unbelievably difficult but rewarding time because you weren't working for your own benefit but for a greater good. That inspired us to take advantage of every opportunity. When the Magazine Publishers Association canceled its meeting in Buenos Aires because people were afraid to fly, we encouraged them to meet in New York, which they did. Others followed suit, like Coca-Cola, which moved its shareholders meeting from its Atlanta hometown to New York. The biggest coup was to bring the World Economic Forum here in February 2002, instead of Davos, Switzerland, where it has always been held. With the 3,500 international business VIPs in attendance, it served to spread the message to world leaders that New York City was open for business.

We took our ideas for morale boosters from all over. One of our most creative programs came from a firefighter who had left the city for a few days to get a break. When he arrived in the small town he was visiting, word spread quickly and soon everyone wanted to meet him. After all he was a genuine NYC firefighter, a true hero. At the Conference of Mayors, held in Manhattan, we announced our plan to have each of the 400 mayors host a firefighter to his or her hometown. The firefighters, who we put on planes, trains, buses and cars, acted as ambassadors all over the country (one even flew to Hawaii). And everywhere they went, Americans greeted them as the heroes they were—and are. They had parades, air shows, you name it. They came back rejuvenated.

There isn't a day since 9/11 that I haven't thought about the sense of urgency to rebuild the city that followed those dark days. The experience made me more grateful for everything— especially my husband, Nick. Walking home from my office on the night of 9/11, I was afraid Nick, a laid-back sportswriter from Kentucky, wasn't going to want to live here anymore. I also didn't want him to worry about it, so I said, "If you don't feel comfortable here, we are family. I will go where you want to go."

"Are you kidding me?" Nick said. "I'm not leaving. We're staying put. We're gonna show those bastards they can't change us!" I was totally in love with this man before, but when he said that I knew I had picked the right one. Amazingly, the ground began to shake. We looked up to see four F-14s fly over Park Avenue followed by fist-pumping cheers from the usually reserved Upper East Siders.

Later that evening walking our basset hound, Gabby, on Seventh Avenue, we passed the Carnegie Deli where the owner, Sandy Levine, was standing outside. "Come in," he said to us. "I have to feed you." I thanked Sandy but replied that we couldn't come in because of Gabby.

"Oh screw that," Sandy said. "You think the Department of Health is shutting us down tonight?"

New Yorkers can be tough, but we can also be very kind and generous. Whenever there was a snowstorm or blackout in the city, there were always reports of New Yorkers helping each other out. After 9/11, the world's perception of the city changed overnight. For the first time, the rest of the country had a chance to see what we are really made of and who we really are.

The Spirit
of New York

The Spirit of New York

Daniel Boulud   Gray Kunz

Charlie Palmer   Don Pintabona

Right after the 9/11 attacks, many people's first reaction was to send food to their local firehouse or police station. Soon, attention turned to the workers who rushed Downtown to search for survivors. Food arrived from everywhere—Chinese takeout, pizza, meatloaf—you name it. But four elite chefs, called "the Four Admirals," figured out a better way. The group included Don Pintabona, of the trendy Tribeca Grill; Daniel Boulud, whose eponymous restaurants have long been among New York's highest rated; Charlie Palmer, who sits atop a nationwide empire of restaurants; and Gray Kunz, a fusion cuisine forerunner at the renowned Lespinasse. These men—used to working with the finest ingredients, the best-trained staffs, the most perfectly designed kitchens—turned the galley of a sightseeing ship named the Spirit of New York into a floating canteen for Ground Zero workers, bringing comfort, and hope, at a time when there wasn't much of either.

Don Pintabona: "Daddy, it's snowing!"

My four-year-old daughter and I were on the roof of our house in Carroll Gardens, Brooklyn, looking over the Hudson River at the horrifying scene taking place at the World Trade Center.

Above us, thousands of pieces of white confetti flew east through the brilliant sky—little shreds of memos, notepads, tissues, the stuff of an ordinary office day, flying on the windless air across the water.

As my daughter ran around trying to catch the pieces, I watched a slip of paper float peacefully back and forth in the sky, until the thing literally fell at my feet. A page from somebody's dictionary that still smoldered, I lifted it up tenderly and blew out the edges so that the white page became ringed in a golden brown, like an ancient document.

My eyes jumped around until they focused on *perverse, perversion, perverted*: a clearer definition of the day's events would be hard to find. It was too much to take in, so I flipped to the other side of the page, now landing on a different word: *persevere*. That jolted me as a call to action as strong and clear as any.

I've got to do something, I said to myself. Somebody's telling me to do something.

In the 11 years since becoming the executive chef at Tribeca Grill, I had passed the World Trade Center thousands of times during my seven-minute drive between home and the restaurant. A mile from my house, 11 blocks south of my restaurant, it was my backyard. I took this all very personally.

I spent 24 hours listening to sirens scream up and down the quiet avenues of our neighborhood and helplessly watched the events unfold from the TV in our living room. Finally, I convinced a cop friend to help me past the 14th Street checkpoint and back into my restaurant.

Dust and debris from the fallen towers coated everything. Inside the restaurant, though, the refrigerators were full of fresh food. There were perfectly marbled steaks and glistening cuts of fish, crisp vegetables and ripe cheese—and none of it would get eaten. Everything below 14th Street—stores, restaurants, public transportation—was shut down. Looking out over the lunar landscape, I couldn't imagine when we'd be back up and running.

There's nothing a chef hates more than waste, so I decided to cook all the stuff and bring it down to whomever I could find who was hungry at Ground Zero. I grilled the fish and meat, sautéed the vegetables and cleaned out all the freezers. I cooked everything until nothing was left.

I grabbed whatever crew had showed up at the restaurant that day and we carried the food to a makeshift triage/feeding center at Stuyvesant High School, a five-minute walk from where the towers had stood. It was an uncomfortable place with a cafeteria of sorts set up next to a triage area where doctors and nurses stood around waiting for the injured to show up. But none did.

We piled the food onto the tables, next to bottled drinks and stacks of nutrition bars, but hardly anyone touched the stuff.

I took a walk down by the Hudson to clear my head. Grim circumstances had turned everything—even healthy and fresh food—ugly. Rescue workers, who would be searching for survivors for weeks under a mountain of rubble, would have to eat or else they wouldn't survive themselves. And Power Bars and water weren't going to cut it. I kept thinking, *"There's got to be a better way."*

The light bounced off the small waves rolling along the Hudson. Another perfect day. A barge peacefully traveled down the river, going about its ordinary business. Then it hit me.

We need boats. Big boats.

Daniel Boulud: Everybody in the restaurant community was stunned and wanted to know what we could do. The scale of the disaster was so big that Lower Manhattan clearly was going to be a rescue and cleanup zone for quite some time. The biggest concern for the chefs, restaurant staff and food suppliers was to nourish those doing the heavy lifting and help put the city back in order in any little way we could.

The Spirit of New York: *Daniel Boulud, Gray Kunz, Charlie Palmer & Don Pintabona*

The day after the disaster, we raided the walk-in refrigerators at my restaurant Daniel to bring food to the emergency personnel, the injured and anyone else in need. The filet mignon that would have gone into the menu's *Tournedos Rossini* and loin of lamb for the *Duo d'Agneau* were turned into over 500 sandwiches and ferried to a collection point. Later that evening, I hopped in a van with two cooks and 300 portions of steaming hot spaghetti Bolognese and rice with peas, corn and ham to see if we could make it to the Seamen's Church on Water Street, where more food was needed.

Although officials weren't permitting traffic beyond 14th Street, I talked my way through—call it French charm or the compelling manner of a chef on a mission. What we found past that border was a dark and deserted city punctuated only by the occasional candle flickering in a window. Inside the church, the scene was no less stark: firemen, exhausted from sifting through rubble, ate what was for many of them their first meal in over 24 hours.

Many chefs around town seemed to be doing similar sorts of quick commando feeding missions, but it was Tim Zagat, a big force in the food industry and then head of NYC & Company, who rallied the troops. He assembled a situation room of about 30 restaurateurs and corporate people on Thursday, September 13, in order to challenge us to come up with solutions to getting sustenance to all those down at Ground Zero.

Don: There was an incredible exchange of ideas. Everyone wanted to help. But how are we going to feed these people?

Then I said, "Look. This is my plan. I've got boats."

After my initial idea the day before of using boats to feed people at Ground Zero, I called a captain friend of mine at North Cove Marina with whom I had been working on a business venture for the last two years. He was building a massive luxury yacht that he wanted to use for catering.

"Vince," I said, "We've got a real problem here. I need the biggest boats we can get—ones with galleys and kitchen facilities. What do you think?"

He knew every boat in New York and what it was outfitted for.

"My friend is a port captain for Spirit Cruises. Let me make a call," Vince said.

We got a rush meeting with Greg Hanchrow, who ran Spirit's fleet of sightseeing boats, and we explained the need for a feeding facility down by the site and a way to get food and volunteers back and forth from some sort of drop-off site.

"Look, take the whole fleet," Greg said. "We've got two massive ships, the Spirit of New York and the Spirit of New Jersey, and several smaller speed boats."

And just like that, we had the boats. Now the problem was the permits. The military had locked down all the rivers, all the waterways around New York. So we had the boats, but we couldn't use them. I worked the phones and called everybody I knew, from celebrities to people in city government. Finally, around midnight, while I was having dinner at Red Cat restaurant with some friends, the call came in that I had received the permits.

"I'm ready to go," I told the group that Tim had assembled Thursday. "I think we can feed 6,000 people a day. We just need the food and manpower."

Daniel, Charlie Palmer, owner of Aureole, and Gray Kunz, the former chef at Lespinasse, all friends, top chefs and mentors, immediately jumped on board, not only with food from their restaurants but with their incredible skills to organize this massive endeavor. Everyone in the industry began *doing*. It was a time of complete transparency; you knew what everybody was about.

We served our first meal Friday, around noon. We moored at the Battery Park City marina, not 60 yards from Ground Zero. Our first ship was the Spirit of New York, a 192-foot ship with four decks—two massive ones that we used for canteens, a third was set up for communications so that people could call home and a fourth filled with cots and blankets so everyone could get some rest.

We had another large boat, the Spirit of New Jersey, at Chelsea Piers. It became a staging area to bring prepared food and supplies and absorb volunteers. It was a gathering place that anyone could reach with messages or donations. A third boat, the Screamer, was a long speedboat for sightseeing that we used to shuttle food and volunteers between the staging area at Chelsea Piers and the ship down at Battery Park City.

Daniel: Chefs get smart very quickly and find solutions to everything. We are very good at logistics by virtue of our ability to transform food from the most simple and primal to the most sophisticated and satisfying. In this situation, we needed to build an organization as quickly as possible, and put some order into the boats. We created team captains and shifts so that everyone knew who was in charge and we could produce food 24 hours a day.

From day one, we wanted to do better than simply offering sandwiches. The workers needed more substantial food, hot food, to keep them going. They were so tired, but nobody wanted to quit.

Charlie Palmer: The galley wasn't much. As soon as Daniel and I walked in there, we attacked the cleaning supplies, got on our hands and knees, and began scrubbing the galley from top to bottom. It would do, but it sure wasn't like the kitchens we were used to working in.

In the very beginning, Daniel was obsessed with trying to do real cooking. I remember he turned to me after I handed him some cooked meat, and said, "Do we have a sauce for this?" I looked at him like he was crazy. *A sauce?* He couldn't help it. He was thinking like Daniel, a creative, master chef. Plus he's French. There's always a sauce.

"No, Daniel," I said. "There's no sauce. It's a grilled piece of meat."

We didn't have time for anything fancy. All we could do was feed people. *Good wholesome food* became the mantra. Daniel became the guru of simple and fresh—and super fast. He ended up being the one telling everyone else, "Faster, faster, faster."

Daniel: I cooked anything I found on the ship—frozen spaghetti (that actually worked quite well) and bags of potatoes. We didn't even peel them.

Gray brought a lot of duck, delicious duck legs. Unfortunately, we didn't have time to confit them. Instead, we roasted them. We roasted (or boiled or grilled) everything. The oven was going 24 hours a day.

Every dish we made, we maximized how much we could do in one pot, and how much food we could get out of one piece of meat or one bunch of carrots. I abhor waste in general, but it was a sin in this situation.

I decided to leave the boat and bring food into the zone after chef Jean-Georges Vongerichten had sent us a 30-gallon cooler filled with chili con carne. He had simply filled the cooler with chili and closed it, so that the entire thing was still hot when I got my hands on it. We had plenty of food on the boat to last for a while, so I wheeled the cooler out to the middle of Ground Zero, at the corner where the towers had stood, and began ladling the stuff into paper cups right there. People were so happy to have hot food.

In my travels in the zone, I saw some guys doing barbecue. Firemen from Brooklyn drove vans into the pit and opened their trunks to reveal hundreds of pizzas. Mamas were cooking as much as they could for their sons, because food is important to everyone.

But our boat was the four-star source. We tried to pamper our guests as best we could, as well as function 24 hours a day. Word got around where the good food was. We had four huge buffets, each about 20-feet long, that we kept replenishing with an ever-changing menu. Almost immediately, we had people who came twice a day, because they knew how good and comfortable it was. That's how fast we built "regulars."

Don: From the moment the first rescue workers arrived on the boat, I was blown away by the image of men and women from all branches of the emergency services slowly walking into our canteen with dazed and haggard looks on their faces as if they had just returned from war.

Some wanted to simply grab a sandwich and get back to the pile as fast as they could. But more sat down to have a hot meal. There were 300 people in all kinds of uniforms—

firemen and cops, National Guardsmen and soldiers from the Army. It was good for them to be in a closed environment where they could set aside what the hell was going on in that vast wasteland of chaos. They lost themselves in the good service, good company and, of course, great food. After Daniel whipped up some meatloaf with prime sirloin, one of the guys came up to me and said, "This is the best meal I've ever had in my life!"

By the time they were ready to leave the boat and head back to the heavy task ahead, all of the workers were hugging and smiling and kissing. And they couldn't thank us enough— and vice versa. We were humbled by their gratitude.

Gray Kunz: These men walked onto the feeding deck carrying the smoke and ash in their clothes and skin. I can still smell it today—the smell of burnt cables, of electrical fire— the kind of smell that penetrates everything.

When you were in that small galley kitchen, you couldn't think. All you could do was push the food into the oven, and make sure it was as hot as it could be. We couldn't afford *not* to have food out at any given time. It's not that we had lunch, dinner and breakfast. It was nonstop 24 hours. There were three or four different ovens, and they were just constantly packed. Wherever we found a slot, food was in there.

Looking out into the canteen of workers silently eating, it seemed like everybody was in a daze. Once, I stepped out of the kitchen for a minute and a guy, completely covered in dust, walked up to me with his dog. The man didn't look at me. He seemed to be somewhere else. I think his dog was guiding him, and not the other way around.

Don: We far exceeded what I thought the boat was capable of, but we had a lot of help—especially from Nick Valenti, who at the time ran the powerful food service company Restaurant Associates.

Nick, who I saw at one of Tim's meetings, ran all the food at the U.S. Open, which had just ended. I told him about the boat, and he said, "Look, I've got tons of food."

"We need it," I said.

Without him, we never would have made it. He got us started with 75,000 pre-packaged meals that bought us three days—because we were going through 25,000 meals a day. People didn't believe us, but we were.

Daniel: The message went over the grapevine about our boat, so all sorts of restaurants and suppliers began bringing food to the delivery point boat.

I called a French friend, Stanislas Vilgrain, at a company called Cuisine Solutions, which produces food for large institutions like the Army. While we had been working on a project to create luxury packaged food, I had tried some sophisticated precooked and frozen penne coated with a sprayed basil, Parmesan and cream sauce.

"You know, I love this pasta," I said. "Whatever you have, send us."

He did just that, dispatching an 18-wheeler full of food with tons and tons of pasta.

But it wasn't just huge companies helping out. Tiny restaurants that didn't produce much food still contributed. Sometimes, we didn't know what the heck we were serving— Indian, Italian, some crazy combo. But we did taste everything.

There was one Chinese restaurant that would send a delivery guy to the Chelsea Piers boat every day around four o'clock in the afternoon with two dozen big take-out bags of fried rice. It didn't matter if it was 10 pounds of food, 100 pounds or 500 pounds, it was still giving.

Don: Oh, God. Trucks just showed up from everywhere. Donations were pouring in from major corporations all over the country.

I have to admit it: I got greedy and took advantage of the situation. I thought, *I can have anything I want.* And about five days into our work on the boat, exhausted from lack of sleep and nonstop serving, I decided I wanted a Krispy Kreme donut. I was just jonesing for a Boston cream.

Casually and selfishly, I told my procurement guy, Jimmy Stewart, "Do me a favor. Find out where the corporate headquarters is for Krispy Kreme. Tell him what we're doing and that we need donuts. Tell him the cops are going nuts.

They need their donuts. Blame it on the cops."

The next morning, a semi truck pulled up from Krispy Kreme. I lifted up the back and it was filled to the top with sweet, crunchy donuts. *There is a God*, I thought. The cops did love it. To this day, if I meet cops or firemen who had been on the boat, inevitably, they'll say, "You even had Krispy Kreme donuts on that thing!" Yeah, well you can thank my selfish ass for that one.

Whatever you needed, people provided. Everyone wanted to help, even those who didn't have that much themselves. An older lady arrived with a hundred brown paper bags, just like my mother used to prepare for my school lunch, with the folded napkin, sandwich and apple. "Please give this to the guys," she said.

One afternoon while I was down working at the delivery boat, a man showed up in a wheelchair and bellowed, "Who's in charge?" After I introduced myself, he ordered me to grab the bag in back of his chair.

"I want to make sure this gets to the people who need it," he said.

I looked inside and there were about five sandwiches and some fruit.

"Where'd you come from?" I asked.

"I live up on 130th Street."

I couldn't believe it. He had wheeled all the way down to 23rd Street—100 blocks—just to deliver some sandwiches. Watching the start of his slow but determined trek back uptown, I had nothing but admiration for him.

Don: For the first five or six days, it was pretty much 24/7. All the chefs slept on the boat—if you could call it sleep. It was more like lying down on a cot for a few minutes. When I finally went back to Brooklyn, I fell asleep on the subway.

It was hard to draw yourself away from the boat. Everybody came on aboard. Friends, colleagues, busboys, stockbrokers, lawyers, all kinds of volunteers from all walks of life. Even the U.S.O. showed up.

"You want us to perform?" they said.

"Yeah, go ahead."

We took pretty much anybody who could contribute.

The U.S.O. entertained while people ate, hoping to add to the rejuvenation and replenishment of the place. One time however, while the girls were right in the middle of a song, a big, strapping fireman stood up and just shut it down. I wasn't sure what was happening.

"I want to sing 'God Bless America!'" the guy said.

Everything stopped. Then the entertainers started singing "God Bless America." And then, two-by-two, five-by-five, gradually, everybody started standing up. By the end,

300 people were standing and spontaneously singing "God Bless America." It was powerful to the point of terrifying.

Eventually my fellow chefs and I had to step aside, hand our operations over to those who could run it long term. About three weeks after serving our first meal on the Spirit of New York, the Red Cross took over what we had started. It was definitely the best, most efficient feeding method around—especially for the numbers we were doing. By the time we left, I estimated we had served around 700,000 meals. The Red Cross offered me a contract, but I refused because I didn't want my efforts to be misconstrued. I was never in the military, so I like to think of that month as my service to the country I love.

There isn't a day that goes by that I don't think about those boats and the men on board. I had the charred piece of paper from the dictionary that floated down on me and my daughter framed, and I placed it above my desk as a constant physical reminder of how lucky I am. Whenever I feel a little down, I'll look at that thing and it smacks me back into shape. It's a compass pointing toward the right thing to do.

Daniel: What has been a lasting inspiration for me was how fast the chaos became organized. In the beginning, the wound those two shattered towers left was stunning. I was overwhelmed by the death and destruction all around and keenly aware of walking on an unimaginable graveyard.

Trucks were coming from all directions in Ground Zero. Offices in the sky had dumped their contents onto the street. Papers were everywhere. I looked down and saw a memo with "85th floor" written on it. Windows and walls were blown out of nearby buildings, revealing bathrooms and other hidden places. It was strange and sad.

Within days, however, there was a makeshift road. People worked in concert, and communication levels were high. New Yorkers weren't overcome by fear and hard work but rather focused on recovery and generosity.

There were all kinds of people taking on responsibility. Some managed safety. Others looked for survivors and, more likely, remains. And others brought supplies or created structures in which the first two groups could work. I fulfilled my role as a chef, and an organizer, by joining my skills with those of others. By gluing all that together, we became the most formidable caterer in town.

Gray: From a chef's point of view, to look at how we could influence that grave time with a half-hour reprieve for the troops when they came on our deck—it was phenomenal. To be able to drop everything you're doing and sit down to a meal, I don't think there's anything more satisfying than that.

When I walk past our mooring area now, there's always a flashback to that moment in time. I see that boat in the water surrounded by the mass of destruction. Then I quickly return to the present—the clean streets, downtown engaged in ordinary business, boats maneuvering the waterways—and I'm again moved by New York's resilience.

Of course, the real heroes are the workers who stuck around, putting their own health at risk to secure the area, find remains and eventually rebuild. But we chefs have an incredibly powerful tool in our hands—and that tool is food. Food is an important common denominator that delivers a universal message in a simple way.

We received so many letters and accolades from firefighters, police and others who dined on the boat. They thanked us for doing something we do everyday: Cook and serve. It was eye-opening to see how healing a meal can be and how it communicates love and care.

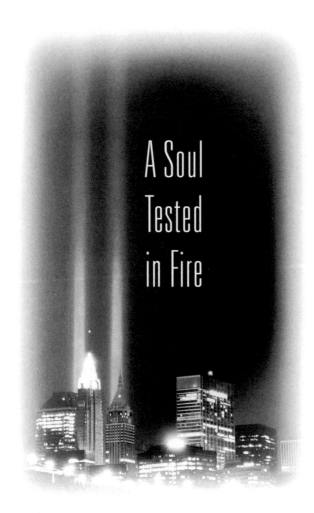

A Soul
Tested
in Fire

A Soul Tested in Fire

Father Chris Keenan

Father Chris Keenan has been a Franciscan priest for 40 years. In addition to being the chaplain at the College of Mount St. Vincent in Riverdale and assisting the homeless in New York City, the sturdy, smiling priest is also the chaplain of the New York City Fire Department—a post he almost refused after the death of his predecessor, mentor and good friend Mychal Judge. But it was Father Mychal who encouraged him to become a priest in the first place, and it was his memory that pushed Father Chris to take up the role as the Catholic spiritual leader to over 11,000 firefighters following the trauma of 9/11.

Father Chris Keenan: After a decade with the New York Fire Department, I still call myself the probie chaplain. A probie is what we call firefighters in their first year with the Department. But a decade later, I'm still a probie. When I first took over after Mychal passed away, people would say, "You've got big shoes to fill with Mike Judge." Although I feel like I'm always learning something new about the job, I never worried about measuring up to Mychal because I know he would have said to me: Hey, Chrissie, don't worry about filling anyone's shoes, or sandals, particularly mine. Just continue to be your good self. Be present for these people. Listen to them in such a way that you hear what they're saying so that you know how to respond appropriately. Enjoy them as much as I did, and have a great life. Pray, be open to God's will and just be there for them, and you'll know what to be, and what to do.

Ever since I first met him in 1962, Mike always encouraged me to trust myself. I was 20 years old at the time and had a teamster job in East Rutherford, N.J., where Mike had his first assignment as a Franciscan priest. Although I was one of six kids growing up in an Irish Catholic family, becoming a priest wasn't my intention. But Mychal, Ben Taylor, an African-American friar, and the others in a local group of young, recently ordained brothers were unlike any other priests I had ever known. They were fun, good with people, happy with their work and, above all, human. I quickly recognized that they had something in their life that I might like in my own.

Mike was the one who suggested I join them.

"I could never do the studies because I cheated my way through high school," I said, but that wasn't my biggest problem. "And how do you spell that word, 'celibacy?'"

"If I can do it," he smiled. "You can do it."

He continued to mentor me after my years of training and my ordination in 1971, when I got my first assignment in East Rutherford to begin a team ministry at his church. Being around Mike was great. He was one of those people whom everyone wanted a piece of because when he was with you, it was like you were the only person who existed. Plus, excitement seemed to follow him. He had a long history of winding up in situations where one wouldn't normally expect to find a priest.

Once while we were in the parish, a man who lived in Carlstadt, the next town over, went off the edge; with his wife and kids at gunpoint up on the second floor of their house, he was threatening to kill them. We arrive on the scene, and Mike Judge, in his Franciscan habit, gets up on a ladder and starts talking to the guy through the window. He told him to put the gun down and that they could work it out, and the man did.

That was typical of Mike, whom we used to joke and call a crisis junkie. He journeyed with the emergency workers and families of the victims of TWA Flight 800 that went down over Long Island. And when a ship, overcrowded with illegal immigrants from China, ran aground in the Rockaways, he was there. He just had a knack for being where there was really a need. Out of the core of his own struggles, ones that people would never know, came his ability to be completely present—physically, emotionally and spiritually. He had a great pastoral heart and a great pastoral sense in that he knew what to do, what to say and how to be there.

So when Mike became the Catholic chaplain of the Fire Department in the early '90s, it just kind of fit. As part of an interfaith team that included Jewish, Muslim and other Christian faiths, he tended to the needs of 11,500 firefighters and 3,000 emergency medical personnel in all five boroughs. Just like a priest of any congregation, he performed baptisms, weddings and funerals, as well as counseling the injured or suffering.

His work with the Fire Department, however, was only one part of his mission. He also helped people on the street, prisoners and others that society cast off. Tending to those in the greatest need was of utmost importance to Mike. For Franciscans, the privileged place of God's presence is always to be found in the poor. And in responding to them, we're in touch with our own passion as human beings, expressing our compassion for the world, and maintaining the integrity of creation by pursuing justice. Mychal Judge was no different than any other Franciscan in that he was a person of peace.

I spent most of September 11, 2001, at St. Vincent's Hospital. Soon after the planes hit the towers, I headed to the hospital in Greenwich Village to volunteer. I stood by the doctors and nurses waiting for the thousands of wounded to appear, which they never did. For the most part, people either got out of the towers before they collapsed, or they didn't survive. The empty gurneys lined up outside the hospital became a more and more unbearable sight as the day went on. I remained there to counsel traumatized survivors or help out with those who showed up with light wounds for as long as I could but left at 5:30 p.m. to walk the 20 blocks to St. Francis where I had a six o'clock confessional shift. In times of tragedy, we often go on autopilot.

I came up 31st Street right on time for confession, but I paused in front of the firehouse across the street before entering the church. Having spent the day at the hospital, I had been shut off from all news, other than the little tidbits delivered by eyewitnesses. I knew something could have happened with Mike: There was no way he wouldn't be in the thick of the biggest crisis to hit New York City.

I walked into the firehouse, where I found somber guys in worlds of their own.

"Have you heard anything about Mychal?" I asked no one in particular.

A young man looked up at me, anger and sadness in his eyes.

"His body is in the back of the firehouse," he said.

One of the firefighters took me to the area they prepared for him and there he lay as still and white as marble. I wasn't shocked—I had a sense that he would be where he needed to be, and he was. The summer before, Mike had premonitions of his own death and talked about it often. He, too, had a sense this would happen.

Even if Mike's death felt expected on a day filled with

unforeseen events, it didn't diminish my sadness. I had been reunited with my mentor and friend in 1997 after spending 18 years in Boston and Washington, D.C., training women and men in graduate schools for ministry. When I asked to be reassigned to New York so I could care for my aging parents, I found myself back living with Mike at St. Francis of Assisi Church. We picked up right where we left off, as good friends do.

When the ambulance to transport his body to the morgue arrived, the friars came from across the street and joined with the firefighters in singing a blessing. Even the gurney's passage into the ambulance, whose doors shut while our voices continued up to that blue sky, felt like a holy event.

Mike was special and soon the whole world would know it. His funeral, the following Saturday, essentially marking the first funeral of 9/11, was aired on CNN worldwide. He became an icon (his death certificate, the first official one, is number 00001), with his own Mass of Christian Burial as a way for all kinds of people to mourn what happened that day.

I'm grateful the Lord took him because Mike would have been absolutely devastated to survive the death of so many of his friends in the Fire Department. It was ultimately a gift that he was able to be with the brothers in their passage from life, through death to new life.

It's good that a priest could be with those people in the lobby of the WTC that day. Why shouldn't one of us be there?

Priests aren't only for counseling in quiet rectory rooms or preaching a homily during Sunday Mass. We must face suffering and fear, no matter the disaster. That was Mychal's final call. You can see it in the famous photo of his body being carried out of the towers. Slumped in the arms of firefighters and police, it is a modern-day Pieta.

That's not an easy act to follow. But someone would have to take over Mike's chaplaincy, and about a month after 9/11, the FDNY asked me to consider it. I said I would, and even went so far as to sit down with the Mayor to discuss it. I wanted to be of help to the department, which had experienced a bewildering amount of death and grief. But I was also anxious and afraid. I didn't feel I could take the job in good conscience because I didn't think I was the right person for it.

I returned home from my last interview—scheduled by the commissioner of the Fire Department—fully prepared to call those who had backed me for the job and tell them to find someone else. I came back to the church and there was Bonnie, Maureen and Michael—the lay team at St. Francis that I worked with helping homeless kids and their moms in the shelters of Harlem.

"Well, we've decided something," the three of them said.

"You actually agree on something?" I joked. "The three of you are the worst team I've ever tried to work with in my life."

"We've decided you're going to do this. You need to do

this, and the firefighters in New York City need you to do this. You've taught us what the Franciscan spirit and spirituality is, with the poor. We're adults. We're trained professionals. We'll take care of the homeless kids and their moms. You take care of the firefighters."

And when they said that, the anxiety and fear moved to serenity and peace. And then I knew it was right. I knew it was God's will and I let go. The next day, instead of saying no, I said yes.

Four days after I was commissioned, the guys in the firehouse across the street from the church, the station Mychal had come out of and with whose men he had died on 9/11, said, "We need to talk to you."

They sat me around the kitchen table, where everything happens, and said, "We know you've given your life for us as our chaplain. What you need to know is, you have 11,000 of us. We know you're ours. Don't you forget every one of us is yours. So anything you need, you say it, and it will be done. If you need a mass mailing done; if you need another person in the office, because of what you do for us, we'll pay for it. We all know you're ours. Don't you ever forget all 11,000 of us are yours."

That's really the way my life is with them, and their life with me. That's just the gift of it.

And I never would have survived that first year without all of them. Quite honestly, it was so overwhelming and so much was happening that sometimes I don't remember the half of it.

In the very beginning I spent a lot of time going into "the pit." Going down the bridge into the work site was like descending into hell, with chemical fires burning and the ashes below our feet made from the death of thousands. And yet, walking through this hell, I saw the face of God on the faces of the people trying to bring some resolution to the families of the victims. This community of recovery showed an incredible level of cooperation. There was great sadness, but also great hope.

And then there were the funerals, sometimes six or seven a day. We had memorial services for most of the 343 firefighters who died. But once remains were found, we did funeral services. As the year went on, more and more remains were identified, so there ended up being over 500 services. I didn't attend all of them, not by a long stretch, but I tried to attend as many as I could to make contact with the family and other firefighters.

My job was nothing compared to that of the firefighters. During that year, the expectation was that in their off-time, they'd help with the recovery. In the firefighter tradition, you always bring your brothers home, so every effort was made to do that. And they would never think of missing a funeral.

The pressure on the firefighters who survived was immense, as was the strain on their relationships and family life. Wives, suddenly realizing how dangerous being a firefighter really is, weren't so excited about their husbands continuing on the job. And the kids would cry because they were afraid Daddy was going to die at work. How do you keep all that together?

As an organization, we had to be careful about balancing care for others with self-care. Some needed psychological or marriage counseling, while others suffered substance abuse problems, easily developed out of that kind of a tragedy. Wherever possible, resources were put toward managing the strain, and also to encouraging a little bit of joy. One tender moment from that year was around Christmastime, when FAO Schwarz shut its doors so that about 800 kids, who'd lost their dads, could have a child's dream of perusing the enormous toy store to pick something out.

For me, I saw my most important role as just being present and letting whatever the need was unfold. "Is there any way I can be supportive to you?" I asked the firefighters time and time again, invoking Mike Judge's calm spirit.

Yes, the strain and grief took a toll on the men and women of the FDNY, but a really great thing emerged that year after 9/11: A resiliency in their hearts and in their lives. The public had a hand in pulling them up. The great majority of people came to see firefighters in a way that they'd never seen them before. These are the persons who run into places everyone's running out of. While firefighters would say, "Well, that's my job," the rest of the world came to recognize them as heroes.

Yesterday was the funeral of Lt. Randy Wiebicke. He was the seventh firefighter who died from cancer that I used to dig with during the recovery.

Twenty-four different toxic chemicals can be found in the lungs of those of us who spent time on the pile. There is jet fuel, asbestos, even DNA from people's remains that we breathed in. I remember while celebrating the Eucharist on a Sunday, right at the pit, the cranes lifted steel and these incredible plumes of green and yellow and red just sort of rushed out from underneath. They poured water on top of it, but with 2,800-degree heat underground, it's pretty hard to douse a fire.

As the years have gone by, that stew of toxicity has had some terrible health repercussions. Like Randy, there's an increasing number of firefighters with various forms of aggressive and debilitating illnesses.

That only adds to the great challenge of finding life in what has been a culture of death. How do the people who survived the realities of 9/11 and those dealing with its aftermath regain a sense of peace, health and well-being? It's a struggle that everyone is working through.

Still, there is life—and a lot of it. Last night, I was with one of the guys and his wife, planning for the baptism of their new twins. Today, I had a meeting with another firefighter and his fiancée about their wedding. Many family members—sons and brothers—of firefighters who died on 9/11 have since joined the Department, which is a remarkable testament to the spirit of brotherhood.

For me, any encounter with the wives, kids, siblings and parents of those slain firefighters is truly special. Whether I'm presiding over a lifecycle event or just coming by for lunch, being with them is always sacred. While their father, son or fiancé made the supreme sacrifice on 9/11, they're the ones who've been sacrificing every day for the past 10 years. Parenting alone. Growing up without a father. Missing a brother or a friend.

As a priest and a human being, I have learned a lot about sacrifice from the FDNY. When you're commissioned as a firefighter, you proclaim to offer your life to protect the life and property of the people of New York City. Just like the police, whenever there's a crisis, you know the Fire Department is coming. At people's most vulnerable and tragic moments, they're there. And any firefighter will say, "It's the greatest job on earth."

Even when it came to their own tragedy—the death of 343 of their own brothers—they didn't run but dealt with the loss and came through it with a new sense of life. Through the spirit and actions of the firefighters, I've seen very clearly that the breakdowns in our life are really an opportunity for a breakthrough to more.

What may be the lesson of the firefighters and their wives and families to the rest of us is realizing that we don't have to look outside ourselves for the wonders that are already within. It's not easy when you're part of a consumer society that says you need something outside of you. But each one of us has been created with everything we need within us. What we can't do alone, we can do together because we are meant to support one another.

Firefighters shouldn't be the only ones who know this, and they aren't. There are many who have been inspired by the hell of 9/11. Stephanie Ali is one of them. She was a middle manager with Xerox in the World Trade Center, until the first tower was attacked and her boss refused to cancel the meeting they were having. That was the moment she decided to do something else with her life and for others. Stephanie walked out of the meeting, the office, the building, and didn't look back.

She became a volunteer with me, working with 50 young homeless men at the CREATE Young Adult Center in Harlem. Eventually she became Director of Vocational Education, and Stephanie's been on staff now for about four years. We've worked together with the staff to create a whole resource and education center for the guys with computers, a library and tutors to help them get their GED, a job, a license, an apartment, furniture, you name it. There is also a mentoring program with active and retired firefighters for the 50 men.

People like Stephanie, a single mom of three daughters who let the breakdown of 9/11 be a breakthrough, echo the message of St. Francis that our life is not for our own sake, but for the sake of others.

I hope that instead of idealizing the firefighters or Mychal Judge that people realize the potential of their own human spirit.

In them, we see goodness and courage shine brightly like gold refined in fire, but those are the gifts of every one of us.

SIDEBAR: *From Father Mychal Judge's Last Homily on September 10, 2001*

> "You do what God has called you to do. You show up, you put one foot in front of another, you get on that rig, you go out to do the job, which is a mystery and a surprise. You have no idea when you get on that rig, no matter how big the call, no matter how small, you have no idea what God's calling you to, but he needs you. He needs me. He needs all of us."

A Teacher's
Education

A Teacher's Education

Ada Dolch

Although she retired in 2010, Ada Dolch still has the direct stare and upright posture of a high school principal. That innate sense of responsibility compelled her on 9/11 to turn her thoughts away from her little sister Wendy, who worked for Cantor Fitzgerald in the North Tower and died in the attacks, and to concentrate on the safety of her students and staff at a public school located at Ground Zero. Nothing she could do could bring back the fun-loving aunt her two grown daughters adored. So, after the attacks, Ada focused her energy on education. Her determination revived her high school from the rubble and inspired the building of another school halfway around the world in Afghanistan.

Ada Dolch: Sometimes the littlest thing can make a big difference.

It was primary election day and our school was a polling place. So I got to school on September 11 before the sun had fully risen to make sure I was there before the first voters trickled in at 6 a.m. The whole neighborhood, including the Stock Exchange and the historic Trinity Church next door, was still quiet before the morning rush.

All the polls were set up, and everything was in order. As the principal of the High School for Leadership and Public Service, we were going to engage in the ultimate public service for our community that day: A democratic election.

When the students arrived later that morning, I returned to the lobby to survey the scene of people voting. There was a man, wearing moccasins and no socks, with a copy of *The Wall Street Journal* tucked neatly under his arm. Another woman arrived with a little dog. These were the prim and proper Wall Street residents who didn't mix easily with my rambunctious teenagers.

I had left my office with my keys, five dollars and one of the school's walkie-talkies, which was powerful enough to keep in contact blocks from the school. I had planned to run to the World Trade Center to get a new battery for my watch, which had died that morning. But before I could run my errand, a power surge blew out the lights in the lobby. As my school safety agent walked out of the building to make sure everything was all right, the lights came back on. I breathed a sigh of relief.

And then *BOOM!*

Our school and everyone inside of it shook with an unearthly crash.

What had been an orderly scene of civic duty a few minutes earlier immediately descended into chaos. Panicked voters ran for the doors. If the Wall Street residents' instinct was to rush out of the building, mine was to stay put.

I have to be with my kids. I belong in my school and nowhere else.

That instinct for responsibility was planted deep inside me as the oldest of six children growing up on the Lower East Side. My parents, Pedro and Clara, had come to America from Puerto Rico to seek opportunity and had found it in factories and the church. My mother worked as a seamstress and my father as a minister. That meant I was the surrogate mother to my younger siblings, making sure they were clothed, fed and out of trouble.

It makes sense then that I ended up becoming a principal and even more that it would be for a school dedicated to public service. I was raised on the value of moving beyond yourself by doing for others. That message was built into every element of Leadership and Public Service's curriculum: Whether studying leaders like Eleanor Roosevelt, Mahatma Gandhi and Jesus Christ or completing the 200 hours of community service demanded of each student annually. We even used the World Trade Center to connect our students to the greater good: Every year, we took the incoming ninth graders up to the top of the towers to see the city from a different vantage point. "Find your community, and see how it relates to the rest of the city," we told them.

One of my students came running in from outside to report that a plane had hit one of the towers.

"You mean like a little plane?" I said. "Like a Piper?"

Nobody knows better than a principal how prone to exaggeration kids can be.

"No, Mrs. Dolch, a big plane."

Out the lobby windows I could see garbage spewing down from the sky over One Liberty Plaza.

"Which tower?" I asked my student.

"The one with the antenna," she said.

"Are you sure?"

That was my sister's building.

Wendy, the second to the youngest of my siblings, worked as an assistant to a broker at Cantor Fitzgerald in the North Tower. The bubbly one in the family, she loved to dance and vacation—anywhere there was hot sun so she could tan her beautiful little body. She didn't have kids of her own but adored spending time with her nieces and nephews, including my two daughters. Wendy was the permanent babysitter and fun playmate.

God, you got to take care of Wendy because I've got to take care of the kids.

After saying my brief prayer, Wendy was plucked out of my brain as if by the hand of God. I had no control over what happened to her, but I did over the staff and students in my school. If I had stopped to reflect on my sister trapped or in trouble, I wouldn't have been able to make the thousands of decisions I was to make in the next couple of hours.

"Oh, my God, Ada, the building's on fire," my assistant principal yelled into the walkie-talkie.

The kids and teachers spread throughout the 14 stories of the school had an up-close view of the terror unfolding from the big picture windows that had made our building one of the most envied in the entire New York City public school system. Debris fell from the tower and, soon, the bodies followed.

The 200 people in my lobby, a mix of students and others who had run in from the street, were now hysterical. Amid the screaming, my mind traveled to two of our students in wheelchairs, another who was 95 percent blind and a last who had just returned from heart surgery. Where were they? I had to get control, even if it meant me getting out of control.

I stood on top of a table and shouted into a megaphone, "Listen to me! My name is Ada Dolch. I am in charge. You're going to follow my directions. If you're going to stay in the lobby, you need to sit quietly. If you can't follow those rules you need to leave the building now."

Nobody left.

Then the second tower, the building closest to us, was hit. This time, we shook like we were in an earthquake.

A huge chunk of something fell right in front of my building. (I later learned it was a piece of the wing from one of the planes.) Now the trouble seemed to have followed us. If steel and concrete could fall from the sky and in front of the school, it could fall through it as well. I made an executive decision.

I'm not going to die in this building. We're getting out of here.

We began a methodical process of evacuation during which my secretary called me through the intercom system.

"The superintendent wants to know who gave permission to evacuate," she said.

"I don't think we can explain it to him. So let's not. Hang up the phone. And I want you out of the office. I want everybody out."

The danger was too close for me. Too close.

Everybody following me out of the building did whatever I told them to. They were happy to have someone give them instructions. I stood at the exit door, and every time a kid came out, I said, "You stay together. Hold hands. Don't be alone."

The plan was to meet at Battery Park, and I kept telling my kids I'd see them there while I waited for the last person out of the building. During that time, my assistant principal was doing a sweep of each floor to make sure no one was left behind.

We pushed ahead. I held up the traffic so that the kids could cross the street. Just as almost everyone had made it into the park, I heard a loud snapping and crackling noise. Turning around, I saw a gigantic wave of black smoke. The South Tower was coming down and headed straight for us.

Any semblance of control I thought I had was lost. This was the end, I was sure of it. I blindly ran, landed on the ground near a bunch of women screaming, wailing, crying and praying, and put my head down on the ground just as the wave slammed into us. Pushing us forward and down, it felt like a million pins and needles running across my back. And then the force kept rolling. But the black stayed.

I squinted through the darkness as little by little light started turning the sky to gray. Ash was falling everywhere. Choking on the ash, I couldn't breathe and desperately tried to clear my throat. And then a miracle: There was a water fountain with a man holding down the spigot. "You have to wet something and clear your mouth out," he said. "Try to gargle and spit." I listened to him and felt better instantly. (After that day, I went back many, many times to look for that water fountain, but it's not there.)

Having regained my breath, I went back on the walkie-talkie and broadcast garbled questions about the kids. *Are you okay? Keep walking.* Thank God, they were okay.

I saw a restaurant I had never noticed before and took

refuge inside just as the North Tower came down. The force of the wave pushed dirt through the walls and cracks in the windows but at least I was in a shelter. Mercifully I found a lot of my kids huddled under the tables. They were crying, even the big, tough boys reduced to little sobbing children, and I thought of all the other students. Thankfully most had gone with teachers on the ferries leaving for New Jersey and Staten Island. But my girls in the wheelchairs?

At around 11:30 a.m., I couldn't take it anymore. We had to get out and move on. I gathered the kids and organized them by borough. "I don't know how, but let's just start walking away from this mess," I said. "If you're going to Queens, you're going to go up the East Side Drive and over the 59th Street Bridge. I'm going to Brooklyn, so I'm going to cross the Brooklyn Bridge."

As I'm sending my fearful troops off to battle, giving them as much information as I can without knowing what we were about to face outside, I felt a small tap on my arm. I turned around and found a little Muslim girl standing next to me wearing a hijab.

"I'm a student in your school," she said. "My name is Sharmeen."

I prided myself on knowing every single person in my school—not only the 600 students and their teachers, but many of the parents of my children and family members of my staff. I didn't know this girl, however, because it was just the fifth day of school and clearly she was a new student.

"Well, where do you live?" I asked.

"Brooklyn."

"So do I. Why don't you stay with me?"

"I'm really scared."

"If you believe in God then we ask God to help us and to push us through. You put your hand through mine like this. We're going to walk together. We're going to be fine."

And we start walking until we got home to Brooklyn.

I spent the rest of the week trying to locate every student and teacher from my high school. And we found all of them. Every kid.

That first night at home, my husband, Norman, handed me the phone. It was one of the secretaries at Curtis High School in Staten Island. "I just want you to know that there are about 300 of your students here," she said. They had mats for the kids to sleep on and the entire community had brought over every kind of takeout imaginable—Chinese, Italian, heros. Blockbuster sent over movies, and the students were arguing about which one to watch. "Good," I told the secretary. "They're doing the normal things kids do."

My mother called, and so did my other siblings.

"Has anybody heard from Wendy?"

No, nobody had heard from my sister Wendy, and we never would. In the days that it would take to find her remains many blocks from where the towers had stood, my only option was to focus on my job and my school.

A lot of people called our house in the following days. They wanted to talk to me because they knew where I had been. But I didn't want to explain or describe any of what I had seen. I just wanted to find my kids.

After I knew my students and staff were safe, my next goal became getting into the school over the weekend. I told myself I had to retrieve all the personal items the teachers had left during the evacuation, but really I was creating missions for myself. I needed responsibility to fill my days.

There was an incredible amount of paperwork and permissions I needed to gather to get into the building (and I'm a principal: I'm not easily daunted by paperwork). Our school wasn't just in Ground Zero—we were in the frozen zone. *Nobody* went there.

But I got the many badges necessary and that Sunday, after church, my husband and I started the slow process to get into my school. It took over an hour of checkpoints and security clearance monitors to finally enter.

Time stood still in the classrooms and offices. A white coat of dust, at least a quarter of an inch thick, blanketed rooms, recalling the moment less than a week ago when we thought the end of the world was near. Computers, coffee cups, wallets, keys and books were like archaeological vestiges of the last normal minutes of our lives. In my office *The New York Times* from September 11 was opened on my desk to news that now seemed trivial.

Of course, time didn't stand still. My beautiful building—where the entire school gathered at the enormous windows to watch the ticker-tape parade for the Yankees wind its way down the canyon after the team won the World Series—had been turned into a morgue. Workers cut out the windows in the lobby to make it easier to drive carts carrying human remains inside. Parts of bodies had been found right in front of our building.

My school had been temporarily crammed into the High School of Fashion Industries where we had to navigate around its 2,000 students. Everyone was angry. Before we had every amenity any teacher could ever possibly want; now we were guests roaming foreign hallways.

So despite protests by some family members and others from the community, I was thrilled when we were allowed to move back to 90 Trinity on February 1.

"That's where *I'm* going," I said in response to the naysayers. "I'm going back to my building."

When we finally reentered our building, it was everything I could hope for. We had so much support: Every student received a backpack filled with supplies; a school in California raised $10,000, which arrived with a huge banner of well-wishes; and people from Japan sent us so many paper cranes, we turned them into curtains. The media covered our triumphant return, our rebuilding of a shattered school.

But it was also hard. Some of the kids cried. We had social workers and doctors on the premises for about six months to treat any kind of illness. Still, there was a flagging spirit that no one seemed able to cure. Many of the kids were emotionally drained by what they had seen and experienced. Some had no desire to do their work or see friends. I heard stories from parents about 16-year-olds sleeping in bed with them like infants.

After explaining the situation to Kathy Ollerton—a successful California real estate entrepreneur I met when she and 17 of her brokers came to New York in March to volunteer at Ground Zero and visited the school after hearing about us on the news—she offered to write a $1,000 check to any senior who graduated. That spring, out of 80 kids, 76 graduated. True to Kathy's word, each of them received a check.

I wanted to thank Kathy in some important way, so I was happy when she accepted my invitation to come to New York City for the first anniversary of 9/11. It was my honor to have her as my guest at the ceremony at Ground Zero attended by President Bush and the First Lady, among many others.

The day after all the hoopla, I took Kathy and a few of her brokers into the Family Room at One Liberty Plaza. It's a special place, for family members of the victims of 9/11, where they can place mementos and pictures, or simply think and grieve. Everybody who has lost someone has contributed something; we go back every year on Wendy's birthday and put up a card. So there's tons and tons of stuff on the walls, in corners, all over the floor. You trip over the abundance of memories.

Oddly enough, the room was empty. Perhaps everyone was exhausted by the ceremony the day before. So we were alone, just sitting on the couch in the unexpected quiet.

"Ada, if you were to leave a legacy for Wendy, what would the legacy be?" one of the brokers asked me.

"I only know education. To me, the only way to salvation is through education because knowledge is power," I said. "Imagine if we built a school in Afghanistan—what a kick in the head to Osama bin Laden that would be."

Kathy went back to California and started raising the funds for a school in Afghanistan almost immediately.

One of Kathy's brokers came from Herat, Afghanistan, and proved instrumental in nudging our project toward reality. We had a strange kind of kinship from the start. One of his brothers had been grabbed by the Russians when they invaded his country and had never been heard from again.

Both of us knew what it meant to have a sibling gone forever in a split second. I think he was honoring both Wendy and his brother when, through his family, he found a plot of land for the school that would teach boys and girls.

Kathy got together the $36,000 necessary to build the school, which the broker had to hand deliver to his notoriously corrupt native country, delivering stacks of cash for construction in person to ensure that it actually went to building something. After many voyages, the school became a reality.

I wanted to go to Afghanistan for the opening. My faith in God had carried me from a time of so much bitterness to a place where I could turn some of it into doing good in the world. The story could be told as one of anger and loss, or as one of hope and life. I needed to check into my own soul and spirit and know that I really wasn't angry at Muslim people. Sharmeen was my first angel. Walking home from tragedy that day, I developed such a bond with this girl that I couldn't be angry with her. I love Sharmeen and carry a picture of her in my wallet as a reminder.

But there was still the small matter of getting to Afghanistan. As private citizens with no umbrella organization, it seemed very unlikely that we'd get clearance to travel to that war-torn country. Kathy made that happen as well. After she met Laura Bush at the 9/11 ceremony in 2002 and told her about my school, one of the First Lady's aides handed her a card. Almost four years later, Kathy used it. We traveled to the White House where we came so close to George Bush we could see him playing with his dog in one of the long corridors. Our travel clearance came straight from the President, and on July 4, 2006, we took off for Afghanistan.

Summer in Afghanistan is unbelievably hot, just brutal heat hanging over the poor, dirty landscape. We were also, of course, covered from head to toe in sweltering black or navy. For a little relief at night, Kathy and I would take blocks of ice from the freezer and put them on our head, letting the cold water run down us as we lay in our rooms guarded by men sleeping directly outside our door so no one could get in.

The security was even tighter as we drove to the official school dedication. Eventually we came to a big red door that looked like the front of an Elizabeth Arden salon, it was so beautiful. After it opened, the caravan passed through and into a marvelous scene. There were so many children and adults, the entire community had shown up. They lined the walls bordering the driveway and threw grass and leaves in lieu of flowers at us while shouting, "God bless America! God bless America!" I don't know who was more overjoyed—them or us.

Behind them sat the school, a bright modern structure of white walls and cheerful blue trim that bloomed from this desert of rubble like a mirage. Inside there was a real floor and sturdy walls. I snapped a picture of myself in the "principal's office." The most impressive feature to the kids was the outhouse. They refused to leave the toilets. It was hysterical to watch. You would pump water into a giant jar, and then use that to flush. They had never seen anything like it in their lives and reveled in flushing over and over.

The school was a godsend (and in turn they thought we were gods). Before, the area had only one school for boys, a three-mile walk each way in harsh temperatures and terrain. Just as we had suffered from 9/11, so, too, had this community suffered when the Taliban came and destroyed their schools. Now there are about 200 local boys—and girls—who attend our school.

The children may have been enthralled by the toilets, but my favorite spot is the garden planted in honor of Wendy. This isn't any big, flashy American garden. It's simply a clear, delineated space with small flowers marked by a sign bearing my sister's name translated into Farsi.

Some things just don't go away:

On 9/11, I was wearing a skirt and heels when I had to jump fences and walk miles home. My feet tired and dress ruined, I thought, *why should we be uncomfortable?* And I haven't worn a dress since that day. But both of my daughters are getting married next year, and I've bought two dresses for the occasions. Maybe it'll be redemptive to show my legs, although the idea of it still seems strange.

And to this day, I still hear sirens and airplanes louder,

I think, than anyone. But I hear them a little less as time goes by.

I still wish Wendy was here. There are constant reminders of her absence. I don't cry when I think about her as I did for a long, long time.

What I think about are the amazing, incredible experiences I have had; things that I've been able to do; messages that I've been able to deliver because of Wendy. There are the hells of 9/11, and they can kill you by destroying your spirit. Or you can take all that feeling and turn it into something positive.

Of course, I'm not thankful she's gone but if her mission in life was over, and she had to go, then she's given me the authority and permission to do something positive for the world.

I know that every time those children in Herat see their school, it is a reminder. The building, completely different in architecture from anything else around it, elicits many questions: "Where did this come from? How did it happen?" Someone will ask the question. And the answer will be, "It was because somebody loved us. Somebody cared for us. Even though there were bad people, there were ugly things that happened, somebody cared for us."

Similarly, once we returned to our school building the February after the attacks, one of the groups that came to provide support to the students was the Working Playground. They sent artists to work with our kids. Together, they created two, 20-foot-high murals that covered the walls in our lobby. (We have since donated them to the National September 11 Memorial & Museum.)

One of the murals was a snapshot of 9/11. There's a fireman wearing a watch with no face because time has stopped. There are the buildings collapsing. There's dust and despair in people's faces. It's dark.

The other is filled with flowers and self-portraits of the students. There's a cross in the distance and birds. Words like "hope" and "life" float through the air in visual poetry. I think that's the future—for both of our schools.

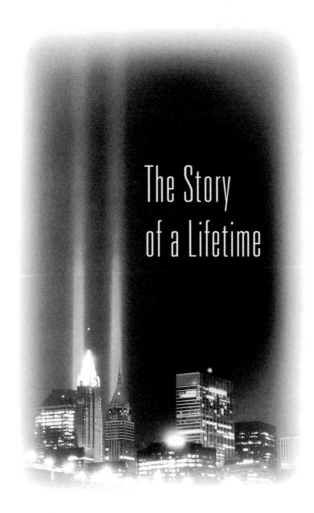

The Story
of a Lifetime

The Story of a Lifetime

Wendell Jamieson

As a new guy at *The New York Times,* Wendell Jamieson was assigned to edit the coverage of those killed in the attacks of 9/11. In journalism, the victim story, however emotional, isn't usually given top billing. What started out as novice territory, however, turned into part of the paper's Pulitzer Prize–winning submission. *The Times'* "Portraits of Grief" brought 2,400 people to life for its readers. Wendell—a 45-year-old Brooklyn native who got his start in newspapers writing obits for the *Jersey Journal*—knew the story was going to be big, but he didn't know it would quite possibly be the most important of his life.

Wendell Jamieson: It wasn't until 24 hours after the attacks that I had my first thought about how we were going to cover the victims. It's a story a newspaper has to do in any tragedy. But how were we going to write about the lives of *so* many people?

I had trouble wrapping my brain around the idea, and not just because, like most of the staff at *The New York Times*, I had worked through the night on coverage of the unreal events of 9/11. I had covered the first attack on the WTC in 1993 for *Newsday*, but I still had a hard time accepting this new horror. Witnessing the second plane hit the tower from the window of my Brooklyn apartment, I grabbed my hair and told my wife that "a remote-controlled plane hit the World Trade Center."

Unable to process the absolutely obvious reality that a jetliner, filled with people, had just crashed into a building in front of my eyes, I had made up a rational reason why nobody died.

"What?" she answered, understandably confused.

"I don't know why I just said that."

At *The Times*—where I drove as soon as I gathered my senses, inching my car through crowds moving the opposite direction on the Williamsburg Bridge—we could only guess at the number of dead. Perhaps as many as 20,000 considering there were 50,000 people working in the World Trade Center, many of whom came to the office early for finance jobs. As a low man on the totem pole (I had arrived at *The Times* from *The New York Daily News* less than a year earlier), I was given the victims stories to handle. While necessary, it's not an easy job: You have to pry into people's lives at the worst possible moment, when families are grieving.

But no story about a death, about a tragedy, will have any impact unless the reader knows who died, and what his or her life was like. We couldn't do obituaries for tens of thousands of people—they'd all blend together—nor could we simply offer a number, no matter how huge, and expect it to resonate.

It was Christine Kay, an assistant metro editor at the time, who came up with the idea of doing small sketches. We wouldn't call them profiles, which suggested a much richer amount of reporting. Instead these 200-or-so-word portraits would focus on *one thing* about each person. We immediately agreed on a page where we would fit as many sketches as we could every day.

This was a once-in-a-lifetime opportunity to do the kind of great journalism I had always wanted to be a part of. Yet, now that it was here, I wished it had never happened.

I'm not a rescuer or a firefighter. I'm a journalist and editor. But, at that moment, we were all New Yorkers and victims. 9/11 had happened right outside my window.

My mind reeled between the big questions. How was I part of the terrible experience of the city? How was I going to handle this professional responsibility?

Where are the names going to come from?

Oh, my God, how the hell am I going to do this?

I didn't even know the vast majority of the people in the

building. But a few reporters, like Jane Gross and Janny Scott, returned to the newsroom with the flyers that appeared all at once around the city, bearing pictures of the missing and phone numbers to contact if they were found. It occurred to us that this strangely universal phenomenon could be used as a database to get in touch with the families of those missing. So a small group of reporters began calling the numbers on the sheets, which was no simple assignment. People at home were waiting for a phone call, but not from a reporter asking questions about their missing loved ones.

But from the first day, readers were moved by the Portraits of Grief, the page's evocative title conceived by editor Patrick LaForge. They recognized the qualities—good, bad, peculiar or poignant—the reporter had picked up on in trying to capture a glimpse of a life. Even if the tribute was small, it was honest.

But we also got pushback from some families, who were confused as to why we hadn't included a traditional obit's information, such as the person's education or surviving children. After the very first page, I received a complaint about the Portrait of a young guy from Queens who had made good and liked living big. A rock 'n' rolling financial guy, he owned a sports car and loved to smoke cigars. Nothing wrong with that.

Unfortunately his brother didn't agree.

"Where's the rest of it?" he asked over the phone.

I explained what we were trying to do with the page: If we

wrote thousands of traditional obits, they would be repetitious and people wouldn't read them.

"There was more to him than smoking a cigar and driving a sports car," he said. "You made him sound like a jerk."

I told him the truth. "Your brother sounds like a great guy to me. Reading this, I thought, 'This guy would have been fun to hang out with.'"

I really meant it.

I got at least one of those calls every week. In a state of great pain and mourning, the families, quite understandably, wanted us to write more. When I described the purpose of the Portraits, sometimes they understood and sometimes they didn't.

To write the Portraits, I recruited reporters from every desk—metro, foreign, arts, you name it. Clerks and researchers amassed lists of the missing and deceased, doling out assignments to reporters throughout the paper. Everyone was supposed to go to the list and pick five names. I wanted to keep it as simple as possible, and after 10 days, the Portraits machine really started to hum along.

The key thing for me was to let the page be organic. I didn't want some neat, artificial well-rounded group of dead people: One head of business, one guy who worked in the mailroom and two firemen. No plan. Just let it all come in naturally. As long as every reporter was seeking that one special thing, I knew there would be enough variation on the page.

That also meant not putting "persons of note" in any special place of privilege either. After filing a Portrait of the grandson of Bosley Crowther, a famous *New York Times* movie critic throughout the '40s, '50s and '60s, one reporter told me, "We have to put this on top of the page. You know, it's Bosley Crowther's grandson."

"It's not like that," I said. "We just mix them all up."

Occasionally, if a Portrait was especially beautifully written, I might start or end the page with it. But I never made any decisions based on a person's job, accomplishments or pedigree. And so you'd have the guy in the mailroom above the guy who was the president of the company. I didn't want to make the judgment that one life was more important than another. Trying to control the page would have produced a stilted feel. It was enough to show the astonishing breadth of loss.

For three weeks, I was totally immersed in the Portraits of Grief, so much so that I almost missed its success. Like everyone else at *The Times*, I had worked since 9/11 without a day off and suffered from the kind of tunnel vision you get when you're part of a really big project. Then something strange happened. Nick Kristof, the op-ed columnist and winner of every award in journalism, popped by my desk.

"This feels like New York's my hometown paper," he said.

It sort of snuck up on me that Portraits was becoming a big thing. Not only did big editors at the paper start congratulating me, but within a couple of days, a number of national media outlets, like *The Today Show, Newsweek* and *NPR* called, wanting interviews. Portraits was the way the city was collectively grieving, people said. Somehow we had struck a chord.

During one of those interviews, I was asked when *The Times* was going to stop running the Portraits.

"We're going to try and do them all," I said.

It seemed to me a reasonable thing to say. As we learned more about the attacks, we realized there weren't nearly as many dead as we had initially thought. Three thousand was still a huge number, but it was doable. At least in my eyes.

The next day, my comment got picked up by other outlets, and it became a headline online: "Times Vows to Profile Everyone Who Died."

"Bet you wish you hadn't said that," another editor commented.

At least my boss couldn't accuse me of not giving the assignment everything I had. To his credit, Jon Landman, the metro editor, let me stay with Portraits of Grief when other editors might have said, "Uh-oh. We have this huge story here, and we've got this guy we barely even know running it." But Jon let me keep doing them.

Despite the fact that I had spent most of my waking hours

over the last month thinking about not much more than the dead, I still hadn't felt their loss. From the minute I had walked out of my apartment on 9/11, I had been entirely focused on getting my job done. Then during my first day off, I decided to attend a funeral for one of the firemen in Park Slope, the Brooklyn neighborhood where I grew up. My wife and I, with our two-year-old son, walked out into a big, beautiful fall day in New York, feeling good about doing our bit to honor our fallen heroes.

The minute the bagpipe and drums started, my throat constricted and I began to sob. It was everything, the crowd lining the street, the sad Irish melody, the fire truck moving slowly down Sixth Avenue with the coffin on it.

Some reporters became obsessed with the Portraits. While 140 reporters from around the paper pitched in, there were a handful who wrote as many as 75 to 100 Portraits. Reporters like Lynette Holloway, Sonny Kleinfield, Maria Newman and Jan Hoffman just kept going, coming in on their weekends and days off to return to the list and take more names.

"I have five more. I'll give you five more," they'd say.

I wouldn't stop anyone.

Regardless of whether the subject was a police officer or a drag queen, whole personalities sprung from single moments. Mike Brick wrote one of my favorites about a 44-year-old firefighter who a broker trainee saw going up the steps of the

World Trade Center as everyone else was going down. It wasn't about the firefighter's life or anything like that. It was just the witness, a broker, describing how the firefighter made fun of himself huffing and puffing up the stairs. The broker helped carry gear up about 25 flights of stairs before the firefighter sent him down ("You stay [a broker], it's better money").

The broker noticed the fireman's name on his coat and pointed to it. It was "Gregg Atlas."

The fireman then bent down to flex, very briefly, like Atlas the bodybuilder.

That was the whole piece, a simple little thing. But you knew him, the kind of guy he was, from that one detail. And he died just moments later.

John Leland wrote a Portrait about a fireman whose wife used to grab his head and smell his hair when he returned from a fire. She loved the smell. It was like a turn-on. And that was it. Oh, it was so beautiful.

The life that emerged in those pages was amazing. Still, we had to work to keep death from creeping back in. Once the Medical Examiner started giving causes of death for the 9/11 victims, a few of those popped into the Portraits. "She was in the second tower," or "He was trapped on the 103rd floor." And once remains were identified, the funerals began and some reporters started quoting the services. I banned cause of death and eulogy speak in the Portraits because there were enough stories in the paper about how these people died.

These are about how they lived, not how they died.

I also had to start watching out for that "one thing," because sometimes the *one thing* repeated itself. For many of the tough, brawling Cantor Fitzgerald guys, the *one thing* they'd always do is go to Smith & Wollensky for steak. There were other *one things* that got banned, like a love of Bruce Springsteen.

The only reporter who absolutely refused to stick to the form was Bob McFadden, a legendary rewrite man.

"To me, what makes someone's life is the totality of it," he said. "You can't boil it down to one thing."

So he did them a little broader. He's a Pulitzer Prize–winning writer. I wasn't going to tell him how to do his job.

Distilling lives down to their essence was a complete minefield. You're talking about 200 of the most unbelievably closely read words you can imagine. Every family member and friend of a person was going to read the Portrait a hundred times. And they certainly came after us not only for errors of fact, which we did our utmost to correct, but also in areas of interpretation.

Another paper criticized us for romanticizing people's lives, but I think we told it like it was. There were definitely some critical Portraits, along the lines of "She wasn't very nice." There were some men who had appeared to have more than one fiancée. There were estranged siblings and others who had problems at home. It exposed life as life is, good and bad. One Portrait told the story of a fireman who started a fire in his own firehouse. The rest of the firefighters, out on another call when the alarm came over, were like, "Wait, that's our firehouse." So we put that in the paper.

Readers really, really cared about the Portraits of Grief. For as many family members who were upset, there were dozens more who thanked us for capturing their loved ones. But perhaps even more gratifying were the many New Yorkers who said they read the page every day, because they *had* to read it every day. When you're used to working in news, a very ephemeral product, that's simply a strange thing to hear.

I received the greatest compliment around the time when we had just started the Portraits. Someone asked me, "How does *The Times* pick the most interesting people?"

"But we didn't pick," I explained. "If you report on anyone's life hard enough, ask enough questions, it's interesting."

We wound down very slowly. At first, we were running one or two pages a day. After January 1, we ran Portraits once a week, all the way through to the first anniversary. After that, I continued to do a few here and there for another year. More names came up. People who had said no at first changed their minds. I had said we'd do anyone who wanted it done, no matter what or when. So we had one Portrait that ran about seven years after the attacks. Out of the 400 people we didn't profile, 200 didn't want to participate and the other 200 we couldn't track down.

There was a point, about six months into the project, when I was still totally focused on it, that I wondered if I could ever get excited about any other story again. 9/11 was a terrible day, and I'm so happy it hasn't happened again, but when I imagined covering an electoral race or corruption scandal, no other story seemed as significant as the Portraits.

In time, however, other good stories came along, and life went on.

I certainly learned a lot editing those stories. To begin with, I learned the subtle and not-so-subtle differences among 140 *Times* writers—knowledge that has helped me as I became City Editor and then Deputy Metropolitan Editor. I got to know some great talents, and made friends. And it made me think about my life. I mean, one thing that came up a few times in the Portraits was people who'd been planning to quit their jobs, but never did. If I'm ever unhappy at work, I promised myself, I will not just sit—I'll do something about it. Of course, I happen to like working here, so that hasn't happened yet.

Occasionally I went back to it—on the fifth anniversary, we did Portraits of families. We decided to do the same thing for the 10th anniversary. But after that anniversary, I'm retiring from 9/11.

Although I'm ready to move on, I don't think there will ever be a bigger story in my life. And yet, it came out of the littlest moments. These approachable 200-word stories generated huge amounts of empathy. When you read about a stockbroker smoking a cigar, maybe you found him annoying or, instead, fun to hang out with; but you knew this guy. We knew him.

SIDEBAR: *The Wall Street Journal on 9/11*

Kyle Pope: The e-mails from the staff of the *Wall Street Journal* starting arriving shortly after the towers fell.

"Jim Browning is okay."

"Peter McKay is safe and in Brooklyn."

"Mike Siconolfi is up and running."

By mid-afternoon, hundreds of people had checked in, an enormous relief given the fact that the *Journal's* Manhattan headquarters, across the street from the World Trade Center, had been devastated by the attacks. In what is still, to me, one of the many miracles of that day, not a single *Journal* employee died or was injured in the attack, though nearly all of us lost friends, sources and neighbors that day.

Our offices, though, were uninhabitable, meaning that the *Journal* somehow had to tell the biggest story of its life without a home and with many of its reporters and editors shellshocked and disoriented. (In my case, a beam from one of the towers blew through my office window; if I had been sitting at my desk at the time, I almost certainly would have been killed.) The fact that we pulled it off—a feat for which the staff would later receive the Pulitzer Prize—is simply one more example of the kind of courage and persistence that would come to define the day.

Out-of-town and overseas bureaus took over editing. Editors like myself worked from home or, later, from a cramped rented office in SoHo. Others were relocated to New Jersey.

But the coverage from those months still stands out as exceptional, even inspired. And while it's an experience none of us would ever have wanted, it's also one we'll never forget.

KYLE POPE is a former editor and reporter of the Journal *and is one of the editors of this book.*

Speaking
for the Dead

Speaking for the Dead

Lee Ielpi

After 26 years fighting fires in New York City, Lee Ielpi, 66, planned to spend his retirement years hunting, fishing, camping and enjoying his children and grandchildren. But all that changed when his oldest son, Jonathan, died, along with the rest of those from squad 288 who responded to the World Trade Center attacks. Lee's response was to help create a Tribute Center at Ground Zero, a first-of-its-kind visitor's center that incorporates personal accounts and those directly affected to highlight the pain, and the hope, of the tragedy.

Lee Ielpi: Six fire trucks were crushed beneath the weight of the north walkway.

That's where I started to search for my son Jonathan.

Almost as soon as the towers collapsed, the place was swarming with rescue workers from every Fire Department around. Nobody asked them to come, but they knew they would be needed and were all over the place.

Everyone was searching the voids, trying to crawl into any space or hole beneath the surface where people could be trapped. The wreckage that had fallen from as high as a hundred stories up was hot from fires that burst on impact and burned for a long, long time. I had arrived in nothing but shorts, moccasins and my Fire Department T-shirt thinking I would be helping on the outskirts. The weather was so beautiful I didn't even think to bring my turnout coat. The hot steel put a burn on my stomach but I kept looking.

I ran into John Vigiano, a retired firefighter like me who had two sons in the department.

"Lee, you didn't see my kids?" Vig asked.

"No." I said. "You see mine?"

I could see in his face that he hadn't.

During that day and night, I kept meeting them over and over, dads I knew looking for their sons, just like me. We quietly asked each other, "You didn't see my son, by any chance?" "No. Not yet."

Like Vig and many of the dads who were firefighters, I brought Jonathan to ride with me on calls many times during my 26 years working for the New York City Fire Department. Like me, he got the bug early.

I joined the all-volunteer department in Great Neck, Long

Island, around 18, and it didn't take long for me to realize that it was a lot of fun going through red lights in a big red truck with a siren. But more important, I liked helping people.

I was sworn into the New York Fire Department in June 1970 and loved every minute of it. Firefighting is a rush. It's a high. It's us versus the red devil. Sometimes things went sour, but even that was exciting.

Both my sons, Jonathan and Brendan, followed me into the FDNY. But it was Jonathan who called me the morning of September 11. It wasn't unusual for him to call; in fact, even though we lived less than a mile apart, he'd call me six, seven times a day, every day, to ask what was going on. "The same thing from the last time you called me an hour and a half ago," I teased him.

"Dad, turn the television on," he said the morning of September 11. "A plane just hit the North Tower."

"Maybe it's a small plane?" I said.

"It doesn't look like a small plane."

"Are you going?"

Jonathan was in an elite unit, one of only seven squads in the city with extra training for rescue, hazardous materials and other special operations. He told the dispatcher they were available. That's a firefighter's nature, to want to go to these big things.

"Dad, we're going to the World Trade Center," Jonathan said.

"Okay, Jon, just be careful."

That was the last time I spoke to my son.

Vig, me and a few of the other fathers looking for their sons turned up at the site early the morning of September 12, and every morning after. There were many, many dads looking but about eight of us stayed together—Bill Butler, Dennis O'Berg, Jack Lynch, John Vigiano, George Reilly, Paul Geidel and Al Petrocelli—who knew each other before the collapse. We became the Band of Dads, splitting into small groups to spend the day searching.

It took three months to find Jonathan. I'm not overly religious by any stretch, but I think the good Lord worked it out. I had just returned home from the site when the phone rang at about 11:30 p.m.

"Lee, we have Jon," the chief said.

Brendan and I immediately headed back down to the site and walked down the horrible little road into the site that we had helped make. Paul, the chief in charge of the site for the night, came up to me and said, "Lee, he's all there." I went over to my son; I had to feel him. I didn't open the body bag—three months is a long time—but I felt him from his toes, right up to his head. And then, in the tradition of the Fire Department, myself, Brendan and a couple of guys from Squad 288 picked up Jon and carried him out.

Among the Band of Dads, I'm the only one who was able to bring his son home as a whole body. (A week or so after Jonathan was found, they found his turnout coat, and then a week after that, his helmet.) Al Petrocelli's family received many phone calls regarding his son's identification. Every time they identified remains, the medical examiner would contact the next of kin. Vig lost both boys: Joe was found but John is still missing. Bill Butler never found his son. Nor did Dennis O'Berg, Paul Geidel and George Reilly. There are still 1,125 missing souls from that day, many consumed by the fires that burned for almost six months.

Three hundred and forty-three firefighters were murdered in a matter of seconds. That's so hard for me to comprehend. In my quarter of a century on the job, I went to one fire where six firemen died, making front-page news across the world. So how the hell could my son Brendan's probation firefighter class lose six of its members?

The only thing that makes all of this a bit easier is that those firefighters loved what they did. Those in Jonathan's company and the other engines and trucks and rescues that arrived at the World Trade Center looked up, and what did they see? They saw what we saw for weeks afterwards on TV—the towers on fire and people jumping. Their mission was to make it up those stairs. It makes it a little bit easier for me knowing that Jonathan died doing what he loved most, helping people.

I was sitting next to Governor George Pataki in his office, waiting to present to him a big idea.

Our group, The September 11th Families Association, began during the early stages of recovery work to make sure families of the victims were kept updated with information from the city. When I joined, I became the organization's eyes and ears. Jennifer Adams, who had a background in investment banking and had worked in the North Tower, spent four months as a volunteer on the site before coming on board in February of 2002. But it wasn't until the spring of 2004 that Jennifer noticed that even though thousands of people were coming to visit the World Trade Center site every day, there was nothing to educate or greet them.

"Let's try and lease that place right next to the fire house, and we can make it a visitors learning center," she said.

I knew nothing about real estate and museums. But Jennifer had a vision, and she's very strong when it comes to what she feels and wants.

So there we were, surrounded by the Governor and many of his staffers, explaining why the state should support the Association in creating a place for visitors who come downtown to understand what really happened on 9/11.

"Let's help them do it," he said, after we finished our presentation.

Then one day not long after, Jennifer noticed something else when a group of about 50 kids came to the World Trade Center from Phillipsburg, Kansas. Barbara and Merlin Dennis, a couple I had met while they volunteered at the site after 9/11, had organized the trip and asked if I would give the students a tour. Jennifer watched how the high-schoolers, who had been fidgeting and fooling around, went completely silent after I started talking about the towers before the attack, about Jonathan, about the recovery work. At the end of the tour, they asked a lot of questions, which I answered as best I could.

Their teachers were taken aback. "We've never seen the kids act like this before," they said.

I laughed. But Jennifer, who had taken a break from her work on the center to join me on the school visit, gave me the kind of look she has when she is cooking something up.

"You know, we should do tours," she said. "We should walk people around the site like you just did."

So we started organizing walks. We kept the concept simple; the 9/11 community would give the tours. Who was better to take groups around the site than people who had lived it? We defined the 9/11 community as anyone who had direct experience to the events of the day. So the volunteers could be someone who lost a loved one, a rescue worker, a survivor who made it out of the towers or anyone who lived or worked in the area.

To date, we have trained over 400 guides, who give five tours a day, every day of the week except for Saturday, when we do six. Our guides incorporate their personal stories into the tour, taking visitors through the history of the World Trade Center—from its creation to its destruction, the events at the Pentagon and of Flight 93 in the skies over Pennsylvania, and finally the future. We don't want to stress our guides, so we limit the number of tours they do a month. We keep a watchful eye on these really great people, who are the lifeblood of the Center. The only rule is that guides are not allowed to use this as a political platform. This is no place for anything other than personal truths, unvarnished.

On a tour, you might hear the story of a woman who can't believe the stupid fight she had with her husband on the day before he barely made it out of the towers. Or the wife who wasn't as lucky but marvels at how her daughters have grown into wonderful women despite losing their father at a young age. Whatever the story, it's real and it gives history a human face.

We have received countless letters of gratitude from visitors from all over the world. We, the members of the 9/11 community, however, are just as grateful to the people who come on our tours because it's just as therapeutic for us as it is for them.

Our society isn't so great when it comes to mourning. There's an expectation that people should move on and stop wallowing. Talking about the dead only makes others uncomfortable. But months, even years, passing don't make losing a loved one any easier. Mourners wind up keeping their memories stored in a tight spot in their chests.

We know that visitors to the Center want to hear these stories from those who lived it. On our tours, it's okay to talk about the dead. We have a mom, one of the many moms, who comes down every Monday. She's a tough Brooklyn lady who told me, "Listen, people I know don't want to hear about my son anymore. My family doesn't want me to do the jabber-jawing when we go out. But you know what? I come here on Monday, and at the end of the day, I go, 'Aaahh.' I spoke to many people today about my son. I feel good because I can come next week and talk about him again."

It is amazing, more amazing than I ever imagined, when Jen was inspired by those 50 fascinated kids. The tours are powerful for the visitors, who come away with a real sense of history, *and* for the guides, who find support and a reason to keep going. We have a commitment to make tomorrow a better day by learning from the past in order to make a positive contribution for our children and grandchildren's future. We are the voices of those who can no longer speak for themselves.

Everything we do is about person-to-person history. When we opened the doors of the Tribute Center in September 2006, each image, testimonial and object was a direct experience of 9/11—just like our walking tours. Bringing out the humanity of this big event is our guiding mission. But it took us a little while to get there.

When we first started building the museum, we hired some amazing professionals. Wendy Aibel-Weiss, Meri Lobel and Caroline Bevan, all at the top in their field of creating personal exhibits, explained to us how you build a museum. There should be explanations of the event and materials helping visitors interpret events.

But Jennifer and I, having witnessed the power of the tours, where the information was personal and unmediated, wanted to replicate that experience in the center.

There was a lot of give and take, and *a lot* of meetings. Seven days a week these people gave of themselves, debating the philosophy behind ideas, the ethical issues surrounding our work, the best ways to have an impact. There were many times we didn't agree. At first I wanted to put something in about the terrorists. I wanted people to know who brought down the towers. But Wendy, Meri and Caroline convinced me otherwise. "Why do we want to talk about the terrorists?" they said. "Everybody knows who did it. Let's just let the people tell their own stories." And so we did.

The galleries take a visitor through a journey beginning on February 26, 1993, when the towers were first attacked, moving on to September 11 and ending with the future. You can hear the voices of firefighters as they went up the staircases in the South Tower. They all died, but their voices didn't. A twisted piece of steel from the wreckage is shiny from all the hands of visitors who have touched it. Jonathan's helmet and coat hang on a mannequin with its back turned as if he's headed to one last fire. One room contains the names of all the people murdered that day—and many of their photos.

The point of Tribute, though, isn't just to cry. We want you to leave with a positive outlook for tomorrow. We have things that'll make you smile, like a photo of two tough iron workers and others hugging and kissing each other after the recovery work ended. We also have inspiring items, such as children's artwork and over 10,000 origami cranes sent by Japanese children and family members who lost loved ones on 9/11.

The point of Tribute is that to stop the terrorists, we must stop hate and learn to live together. Hate is the easiest thing in the world to do. I'm not going to tell you I didn't have hate on 9/11, 9/12 and 9/13. But what is it going to get me? Not justice, which is what I want.

That's a lofty goal, and one we weren't sure we could achieve through our little center. So we put cards on the table in the last gallery on the very first day asking people to share their thoughts on what they had seen. We weren't sure what we'd accomplished. More than 200,000 cards from over 135 countries later, messages of beauty, reaching out interesting ideas, and hope for peace don't stop. Just when I think I've seen everything—pictures of the towers artfully turned into peace signs or meaningful poetry—another card comes along to surprise me. What's truly remarkable is that out of all those thousands of cards, there are maybe 10 that we've received with some expression of hate in them.

Our message is one of positive change. No matter how small or insignificant it might seem, do something to make tomorrow better. That's what we want people, especially young people, to learn. Unfortunately, our country has failed when it comes to educating kids about the events of 9/11. There might be a chapter, or a paragraph, about the day, but there's not a state in our country that has a curriculum to teach the history of 9/11. So we're taking our message to schools with a teachers' resource, a series of videos that show how easy it is to hate but how positive action is much more powerful. As with our walking tours and galleries, our teacher tool kit has real people telling their beautiful, powerful stories of turning anger into building schools in Afghanistan, creating advocacy organizations for Muslims living in New York City or giving walking tours through Tribute.

While this is definitely not what I had planned for my retirement, I feel like we are making a difference. I can't bring back my buddy and son Jonathan, but I can do something for my other children, grandchildren and all the kids of the world.

SIDEBAR: *The Guides*

Anthony V. Palmeri, who worked for the NYC Department of Sanitation for 23 years, volunteered for nine months cleaning up Ground Zero.

Why do you give the tours?

It's important that everyone knows what happened that day and what has happened since that day. 9/11 was indeed a tragedy, but it also brought out the greatest show of love and support for those left behind. Over these past 10 years, I have learned what it is to be compassionate toward the misfortune of others. I feel honored to have played a small part in something much more than I could have ever imagined.

Is there anything particularly difficult in leading them?

Talking about myself. There were so many people involved—firefighters, rescue workers, survivors, people who had to deal with the hard part. As a sanitation worker, my story is relatively small. When I talk about myself, I get an uneasy feeling because it's not about me. It is about 9/11.

So why do you continue to volunteer?

It is constant therapy. I have to remember the goodness that came out of 9/11. It helps me heal inside. I have a need to talk about it and tell others. The attack was the worst experience of my life, but being a volunteer has been the best experience of my life.

What's the best part of the tour?

At the end when people come over and hug you. When they appreciate what you do and thank you, that's very special because I know I've made myself understood.

Shari Hartford, a magazine editor and longtime Battery Park City resident, was shopping in the World Trade Center when the first tower was hit.

What is one of the most common questions you get on your tours?

Everyone wants to know what it was like when the towers collapsed. My husband, Bill, and I had reunited in our Battery Park City apartment when they came down. It was like a freight train, volcano and earthquake all combined, times 10. Our 17th floor apartment faces the river, and the first thing we saw was thousands of pigeons fly by, then we were enveloped in the cloud and you couldn't see anything. I took my purse and our little dog and we left. We were evacuated by tug boat to New Jersey, and we weren't allowed back into our home for five weeks. The whole neighborhood was a crime scene.

How did you become a part of the Tribute Center?

I used to hear one big shot in a group of tourists saying, "I know what happened here," and think, *God, they don't know anything.* If I was in the mood, I would say, "You are full of shit." Then I started thinking there must be a better way of getting this information out. I saw an ad in a Battery Park City paper that Tribute was looking for volunteers, and that was it.

So you've been successful in telling the story of 9/11?

My favorite part is putting a face with the story. That's what Tribute does. When you go home to wherever you are from and you are telling the story, you will be able to say there is the little gray-haired Jewish lady from New York and this is what happened to her.

Brenda Berkman, a Lieutenant in Chelsea's Ladder Company 12 on 9/11 who retired from the FDNY in September 2006 as a Captain, was off duty when the attacks happened but made it to Manhattan just as the North Tower fell and remained working at the site through April.

What's the 9/11 story you bring to visitors?

My main motivation in giving Tribute tours is to honor and remember the people who lost their lives and were injured on 9/11. I also try to give people awareness that there were women rescuers working down there alongside men, which was left out of the picture portrayed by the media. Three women rescuers were killed during 9/11, many were injured and many more responded afterwards. Women were doing all the things that the men were doing. Americans, both women and men, were united in their desire to serve their country. When people see me and hear my story, they know for a fact that women were there.

That's a powerful message, which must feel pretty good to tell.

At the same time, telling about the suffering and the hard times brings back a lot of emotion. I lost a lot of friends. Most of the time that's very difficult. It brings back the memories that time passing tends to diminish. I don't want to forget about the enormous sacrifices that were made, not only by those killed but also people who were injured and lost their health working down there. Americans have very short-term memories when it comes to historical events, but we shouldn't forget that.

Do you learn anything on the tours?

Hearing stories from the other docents is important to me. Sometimes the visitors share stories about their connections with 9/11 or other traumatic events. We get a lot of British and sometimes people from the Middle East, who explain what it's like to live with the constant threat of bombings. The message Tribute promotes is to make the world a better, more peaceful place.

Désirée Bouchat—who worked on the 101st floor of the South Tower for an insurance brokerage firm that lost 176 employees, including 19 on her floor—left as soon as she realized a plane hit the North Tower and had taken about 10 steps out of the building before the second plane struck her tower.

Did you have any reservations about volunteering at Tribute?

I wasn't sure I could do tours because I'm not good at public speaking. But I learned that I can do public speaking when it's something I'm passionate about and is meaningful. This is definitely meaningful.

Meaningful and moving.

I did a tour with a docent, who didn't talk about how 9/11 affected her. She talked about the children. "Who are the children of 9/11?" she asked. Everyone thinks about the children who lost their parents, but she read the names and talked about the nine children lost on the airplanes. That was one of the more moving memories. The smallest victims.

That is very sad.

I did a tour where one of the guests had lost her husband in the 2004 tsunami. My fellow docent on the tour had lost her firefighter husband in 9/11. I listened to the two of them converse. "I noticed you are not wearing your wedding ring," the tourist asked the docent. "When did you take it off?" It was so hard for me to hear, but the two of them seemed fine. They were making a connection.

Eileen Lugano, a teacher who raised her children in New York City, lost her 28-year-old son, Sean, who worked as a stockbroker in the World Trade Center.

How did you find the strength to start giving tours?

The September 11th Families Association, which served as a clearing house of information for those of us directly affected by the events of 9/11, reached out to us around 2004 to volunteer to give tours of the WTC site. At first, I ignored the request. After a few more requests, I decided to give it a try. Lee Ielpi gave the initial tour to those of us who volunteered at that time. It was somewhat emotional for me and I thought I'm not going to do this. *This is crazy!* But then I came back. I did it and continue to do it now to keep my son Sean's memory alive and to have people remember the great loss New York City suffered.

What's the hardest part for you?

The hardest part is my personal story. I tell it at the third stop. I talk about my experiences and fears on that day. I talk about the search for Sean, who worked on the

89th floor of Tower 2 and the many, many people who joined us. I talk about Sean, my perfect child, but I avoid the emotional toll and the tremendous loss my family suffered. Some people on the tour will ask questions about Sean, what he was really like. I don't want to cry. I must decide what the boundaries are. There are times I wish I could talk more about him.

Why is talking about it important?

There are many who do not talk about what happened on that day. Those are the people we should be concerned about. Twenty-five thousand people ran for their lives, and we don't hear too many of their stories because it's too painful. But keeping all that in has to be very hard.

You give four tours a month? That's a lot.

I actually try to do one a week, if possible. I now look at my tour not only as a way to keep Sean's memory alive but also as a way to celebrate him. At the end of my personal story, I show pictures of my seven grandchildren all born after September 11, 2001. There is a message. Life goes on. Joy does return. But we must always remember what happened here.

New York Says Thank You

Jeff Parness

One small fight between his sons over a toy inspired Jeff Parness to come up with a big idea to thank the rest of the country for helping New York on 9/11. He started *New York Says Thank You*, which takes volunteers every year to build projects for towns devastated by natural disasters on the anniversary of the attacks. What started as a way for Parness to teach his kids a lesson on philanthropy has turned into an annual opportunity for survivors of 9/11 and other tragedies to rebuild houses—and their own spirits.

Jeff Parness: One day I found every person in the town of De Gonia Springs, Indiana, lined up to give me a hug.

I was in the small town outside of Evansville on the fifth anniversary of 9/11—along with about 600 volunteers (double De Gonia's population) made up of New York City firefighters, Ground Zero workers and other survivors of catastrophic events across the country—to rebuild Baker

Chapel, a 140-year-old church that had been destroyed in a tornado a year earlier. The night before, we framed the 9,000-square-foot church. It had been like a family reunion. Those of us who get together every year on 9/11 to do a building project like this one partied until five o'clock in the morning, knocking back beers and catching up on a year's worth of news. Showing up at the worksite the following morning with a bunch of New York City firefighters to start building with 50 local Amish guys was kind of an interesting cultural exchange.

"God bless you for doing this," a young woman outside the new church said before hugging me.

I looked at the woman and told her what I had told everybody else.

"We're just doing what people did for us," I said. "You want to thank me, show up next year at the next town we go to."

Repaying the Americans who traveled to New York City from all over the country to lend a hand when we needed it most or who sent money, cards, handmade blankets, socks and support in any shape is the essence of "New York Says Thank You."

But it started with a fight over a toy: My two sons, Evan, five, and Josh, two, amped up from all the sugar they had eaten the day before on Halloween, were bickering about a stuffed animal when I completely lost it.

"You've got hundreds of stuffed animals," I yelled.

It was the first time I had ever raised my voice at Evan. I went into the other room and turned on the television to chill out. CNN was covering the terrible Southern California wildfires of fall 2003 that had wiped out the homes of 3,300 families in a matter of days. A mother from San Diego described how there had been trick-or-treating in the shelter, but her daughter's Sleeping Beauty costume had burned up along with their house.

I decided to bring Evan, who had worn three costumes to trick-or-treat in our 35-story apartment building on Manhattan's Upper West Side, into the living room to tell him about the wildfires and teach him a lesson.

"All these people just lost their homes, and this little girl lost her Halloween costume. Meanwhile you wore three yesterday," I said. "What would you do to help a girl in that situation?"

He got very quiet and then said, "Maybe we could put some of the toys I don't play with—and maybe some of Josh's, too—in a box and mail them to the mother to give to the girl."

"What if you collect toys from all the kids in the building that were at the Halloween party last night?" I asked.

"Oh, Dad, we could send lots of stuff to the kids in California."

What had I gotten myself into? I wanted to teach Evan the value of giving, but there were *a lot* of families in this building and most of them had plenty of stuff they'd be willing to give away. If we ended up with 35 boxes, it would cost me an arm and leg to send across the country. It would probably be cheaper to rent a truck and drive it there myself. And as soon as I had the thought, I realized what an incredible statement that would be as a father.

Then I had another thought. I had just been listening to Mayor Rudy Giuliani talk in the press about how people were forgetting about 9/11. The lessons and goodness that came out of it were already beginning to recede into memories not more than two years later. I hadn't forgotten. I had lost my business partner, Hagay Shefi, who had been at Windows on the World; a day didn't go by when I didn't think about him.

We're going to drive a truck across the country with a big sign that says, "New York Says Thank You."

Evan loved the idea. (What kid doesn't love a plan that involves a truck?) Within a day we collected far more than 35 boxes worth of stuff. Tenants throughout the building helped tape up the boxes and get them ready to transport cross country. I had never done anything community-service oriented in my life, but I felt like I was on fire. My heart didn't stop racing from the moment I had the idea to less than a week later, when two friends and I started out from 96th and

Broadway with a U-Haul (paid for with donations by great neighbors like the local chicken store owner Arturo Canela) filled with relief supplies for the California fire victims.

The big sign on the side of the truck, "New York Says Thank You," became a rallying cry as we crossed the country on our way to our destination.

As I talked to people at rest stops, gas stations, diners and malls about their memories of 9/11 and what they did to help New Yorkers, I realized that we were doing this not because of what happened on 9/11. We were doing it because of what happened on 9/12. When everybody from small towns and big cities, all across America, came to New York to help us in our time of need, it changed New York and me personally just as much as the attacks did. We realized we were not invincible, and also that we weren't alone.

Delivering supplies to people in San Diego reignited those memories of unity, and I decided that was something I wanted to experience every year. So after returning to New York, I turned my trip to California into a plan to use the 9/11 anniversary as a way to build stuff, an annual attempt at reversing the destruction of that day.

On July 19, the day after I incorporated the foundation, I walked outside my building and saw an FDNY battalion command truck parked across the street. While I had been thinking about what "New York Says Thank You" could become, there had been growing press about the lingering psychological impact of 9/11 on New York City firefighters. Many of them were clinically depressed and yet few of them were seeking counseling, according to reports. I knew it was inherently cathartic to use the 9/11 anniversary as a way to do something positive with a physical impact, and I thought it would be really cool to get the effort connected to the Fire Department. But I didn't know any firefighters.

So I walked right up to the command truck and introduced myself to a six-foot-seven Irish guy, who turned out to be Chief Michael McPartland from my local firehouse. I explained my plan to return to California in a couple of months to build a house for a family displaced by the wildfires.

"Why don't you get me five of your guys? We'll figure out a way to fly them to Southern California to swing a hammer on 9/11. We'll go put up a house as a way to say thank you."

He did, and on September 11, 2004, we took 14 volunteers from New York (including 11 New York City firefighters, three of whom were in the North Tower when the South Tower collapsed) to Harbison Canyon, a California town that lost 75 percent of its homes in the wildfires. When we got there, the whole town showed up with barbecues and bagpipes. It was the most American thing I'd ever been privileged to attend. Firefighters from all over Southern California arrived to help us build a house. That's how the whole thing started, with 14 volunteers and the frame of one house. Seven years later, we have over 1,200 volunteers who can build three houses and a community center in a weekend.

The secret sauce to "New York Says Thank You", the reason this thing keeps getting bigger even as we get further away from 9/11, is because it's not about 9/11; it's about commemorating the sense of community, humanity and kindness that followed the attacks, when people came together to help each other.

Our core group has always been New York City firefighters, probably half of them survivors of the Trade Center. But there are also Ground Zero construction workers; 9/11 family members; New York City school kids, who take off the first week of school with their teachers and parents to come with us; employees from the buildings surrounding the Towers, who watched people jump. To all these people, getting together on 9/11 to double the population of some small town nobody's ever heard of and do barn raisings is therapy.

The first year Pia Hoffman, who operated the tall tower crane that picked apart the debris pile at Ground Zero, came with us when we traveled to Groesbeck, Texas, a small town east of Waco that was hit by a tornado. On the second day of building a house for the Vincents—three generations of a family that cared for disabled veterans out of their home destroyed in the tornado—I watched Pia operate the crane to build the roof.

As she set upon the roof with her crane, I thought about this woman, who for nine months got in a crane to pick metal off of body parts. Now she was building something for strangers on a dusty road in the middle of nowhere.

That night, over beers and barbecue, I asked Pia about that image.

"Do you have any idea what that represented?" I asked.

Pia is probably one of the toughest women on the face of the Earth. The Germany native hangs out with steelworkers all day and works in a crane 400 feet above New York. She's not exactly what you would call the emotional type.

"What do you mean, *represented*? I'm here to do a job," she snapped.

I didn't push it with Pia, but a couple of weeks after the trip I saw her and she threw her arms around me.

"That trip to Texas finally let me put 9/11 behind me," she said. "I'm coming on these trips for the rest of my life."

I'm thankful that so many professional builders like Pia love coming with us every year. A lot of the firefighters we bring to a town are often part-time carpenters, but we usually have about 80 professional construction workers—managers, carpenters, tradesmen—on any given project. Guys like Charlie Vitchers, the construction superintendent for the cleanup at Ground Zero, who builds skyscrapers when he's not pulling apart debris piles. He is the reason we can tackle a big project like the one we did in Greensburg, Kansas.

On my first visit to Greensburg, a historic town that was 95 percent destroyed by a massive tornado, I asked one of the pastors in charge of the recovery about the community's greatest need. Part of the formula, when we go to these places, is to figure out how we can make the most impact: Build something for a special family where, if we help that family, it will bring the entire community out to create a network around them; or build something that will benefit the entire town.

The pastor reiterated a common refrain.

"The tornado destroyed the social fabric and the social glue because now there's nowhere for people to be together," he said.

"Whatever we build has to be the glue factory," I said. "It has to create even more glue."

A couple of months later, they came back to us with their glue factory: A 4-H barn. I'm a Jewish kid from New York. What the hell do I know about 4-H? But I quickly learned it's the place of county fairs, where many generations and many towns gather in this heavily agricultural area.

The weekend of September 11, 2008, about 250 of us showed up in Greensburg to build a 14,000-square-foot barn. We planned to build the entire thing in three days, but pouring rain had us working in three feet of mud, so we got about

60 percent of the framing done. What's amazing is, people from the surrounding communities, who heard about these New Yorkers trying to help on the 9/11 anniversary, stepped in to finish what we started.

The spirit of volunteerism spreads quickly. Not only do we take more New Yorkers on our trips every year, but people from all the small towns across the United States that we've helped on previous anniversaries of 9/11 keep showing up with us to pay it forward by helping the next community in need.

When we bring New York City firefighters and others who survived 9/11 to these towns, where they're in the throes of their own disasters, we are transforming their consciousness. Arriving in places like De Gonia Springs with guys who represent the greatest tragedy in modern American history enables the town residents to see past their own tragedy. They realize they're not victims; they're survivors.

"You guys survived, just like we are going to," they say. "Next year, we'll be marching by your side down someone else's Main Street."

"New York Says Thank You" keeps growing because what we're really doing is empowering survivors as volunteers by taking what could be their worst day and turning it around.

No project embodied the transformation of tragedy into hope better than the Little Sioux Boy Scout Camp in Western Iowa.

About 50 miles northeast of Omaha, Nebraska, the Boy Scout camp was hit by a tornado that killed four kids. What happened there was a tremendous story of service and sacrifice with older kids rescuing younger kids as best they could. For the 9/11 anniversary in 2009, 1,200 volunteers arrived to rebuild the camp, with about 300 from New York and the rest from previous projects and members of the scouting community in three states. Our main project was to build a chapel on the foundation of the bunk where the boys had died in the tornado.

Using trees destroyed by the tornado to create the beautiful structure of the chapel was hopeful in itself. But even more so was the closing procession on Sunday morning. At every project we have a closing procession where members of the FDNY, in their dress blue uniforms, march to bagpipes at the front of the parade of volunteers.

For the closing procession at Little Sioux, we interspersed the kids with the firefighters. The scouts who had survived the tornado that night were marching shoulder-to-shoulder with all the FDNY guys to show the parents of the kids who survived and those who lost their boys, as well as the kids themselves, that like the greatest heroes of 9/11, they, too, have what it takes to move forward.

A couple of weeks before we went to Greensburg, Kansas, to help rebuild the barn in 2008, I got an e-mail asking if

I could bring a remnant of the Trade Center to create a Veterans Memorial Park in the town. I knew Charlie had pieces of steel and stuff like that, so I paid him a visit at his construction site at 55th and Eighth. After relaying the request, he said, "I have got steel, but I've also got the pieces of this 30-foot American flag that was destroyed."

The flag, immortalized in a famous photo, had hung at 90 West Street, the heavily damaged building directly south of the Trade Center. Flying from the scaffolding during the eight months it took to clean up the site, the flag became a shredded symbol of the country's patriotism. Charlie sent a crew of construction guys to rescue the remains of the flag in October 2001 in order to have it honorably retired. When we talked in 2008, he still hadn't figured out the protocol for retiring the flag.

"Well, why don't we just bring it back to life?" I said.

Turning something torn into something whole is the essence of what we do at "New York Says Thank You."

In Greensburg, Charlie dropped the 13 pieces of the flag off at the senior citizens center where the ladies of the town laid them out on a table and set about stitching them back together. Not all of the original flag was there, because some of the fabric had torn away or been burned off. So where the pieces of the original flag were missing, on their own, these ladies decided to sew in American flags that had survived the

Greensburg tornado. The material didn't always match up, but it was beautiful.

They created a new piece of American history in that senior center. What was destroyed in the aftermath of the World Trade Center in New York was brought back to life seven years later by folks who survived the worst tornado in American history. To me, that's what America's about; we're all there for each other.

Thinking about the 10th anniversary of 9/11, we know there are so many things we will never be able to make whole again. But we could make the flag whole again. So the "New York Says Thank You" Foundation embarked on a 50-state National 9/11 Flag Tour to do just that. We've been taking the flag to all 50 states, where military veterans, first responders, schoolteachers, kids, community service volunteers, 9/11 family members and the general public are stitching the flag back to its original 13-stripe format to make it whole again by the 10th anniversary.

We've had World War II veterans who survived the USS Arizona stitch the flag in Hawaii on Pearl Harbor Day. We had Martin Luther King Jr.'s family stitch the flag on Martin Luther King Day. We've had soldiers and school kids at Fort Hood, Texas, stitch the flag right around the anniversary of the shooting. The family of Christina Taylor Green, the little girl born on 9/11 who was killed by a gunman in Tucson, flew the flag at her funeral.

In the stitching ceremonies, we make patches using fabric from American flags being retired in all 50 states. Part of the restoration effort means taking off some of the Greensburg flags to match the original colors of the flag, but there is some amazing history stitched into the new flag. Pike County Historical Society in Milford, Pennsylvania, donated a piece of the flag that Abraham Lincoln was laid on and bled into after he was shot.

The story this flag will tell when it's completed and becomes part of the permanent collection of the National 9/11 Memorial Museum isn't about what happened on 9/11; it's going to be about what happened on 9/12. The flag exists, and is even more beautiful than it was originally, because of how many people are connected to it. This is what it looks like when Americans come together to help each other recover.

People often ask me, "How do you deal with thinking about 9/11 so much?" But I don't think that much about 9/11. I think about how you extract the positive that came out of it. How do you capture that in a bottle, store it, shake it up every year and sprinkle it around a community in need? You do that through action. You do that not just by remembering the loss, but by building something.

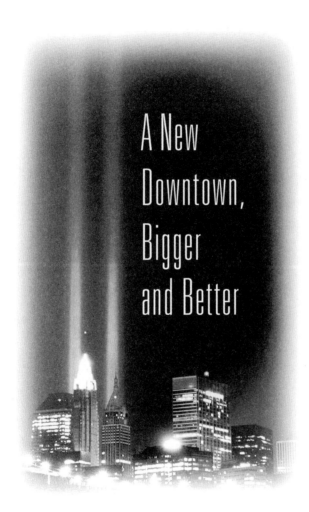

A New
Downtown,
Bigger
and Better

A New Downtown, Bigger and Better

Elizabeth Berger

Downtown Alliance President Elizabeth Berger lived across the street from the World Trade Center site. When the planes hit, she saw what happened in real time. In her words it was "terrible, unthinkable, impossible." Those buildings weren't made to come down. The sheer volume of dust covered everything for blocks around with the buildings' remains piled seven stories high creating a ghastly picture of utter devastation.

Elizabeth Berger: Now it's a 180-degree turn. It is more than just rebuilding. Lower Manhattan has arrived as a new kind of place to live, work, go to school or visit.

The 16 acres that make up the WTC mean many things to Americans. To me—someone who lived here before the attacks and returned to my apartment four months afterwards—the site is not only a reminder of man's occasional inhumanity but also of our profound goodness. People gave so much of themselves here, whether it was the unbelievable bravery of the firefighters and police officers rushing in to the burning buildings or the regular New Yorkers who returned to work or live in the area. The NYPD, iron workers and other volunteers heroically did an unprecedented job of clearing the site ahead of schedule.

Since then, the WTC has been the site of one of the most complex engineering jobs in the world. One has to understand the scale of this project to appreciate it; more office space was lost at the WTC site on 9/11 than exists in the whole city of Atlanta. As Port Authority Executive Director Chris Ward once said, the rebuilding has been like a lasagna of layer after layer after layer of individually complex projects. That's all while 306,000 people come downtown every day to go to work, 56,000 others live or attend school, millions visit from all over the world and subway trains continue to run through the site.

I never talk about "Ground Zero" because this militaristic and clinical term has nothing to do with the tremendous vitality that is happening here. The rebirth of the World Trade Center and Lower Manhattan is an incredible engineering, political, architectural and human achievement. It should be a symbol for all Americans of resilience, strength and determination.

To understand the extraordinary scope of rebuilding since 9/11, all one needs to do is come down and see the new towers rising. It is anticipated that the new downtown will attract nine million visitors a year. In fact, I think it's obvious that downtown will be truly bigger and better than it was on September 10, 2001.

SIDEBAR: *Here are a few statistics concerning the new World Trade Center:*

– All told, the site covers over 16 acres.

– The cleanup after 9/11, initially estimated to take two years and cost $2 billion, was completed in nine months for $650 million.

– Since 9/11, $30 billion has been dedicated to reconstruction in Lower Manhattan.

– When completed, the WTC area will include a series of skyscrapers comprising seven office towers with 14 million square feet of office space and 550,000 square feet of retail space.

– Such world-renowned architects as Santiago Calatrava, David Childs, Norman Foster, Daniel Libeskind, Fumihiko Maki and Richard Rogers have worked on rebuilding the WTC. Also, Michael Arad and Peter Walker worked on the National September 11 Memorial and Museum.

– One World Trade Center, aka the Freedom Tower, when finished, with its antenna mast, will reach 1,776 feet, making it America's tallest skyscraper.

– In May 2006, real estate magnate Larry Silverstein opened 7 World Trade Center with 1.7 million square feet of space.

– Towers 2, 3 and 4 are in construction.

– Now at full occupancy, Goldman Sachs' new 43-story headquarters houses 9,000 workers.

– The state-of-the-art WTC Transportation hub will serve 250,000 people a day.

– A new Performing Arts Center will house the Joyce Dance Company.

– Eight acres make up the National September 11 Memorial, including a Museum containing an extensive collection of artifacts, ranging from monumental pieces of WTC steel to personal stories and mementos.

– The Memorial will be planted with hundreds of oak trees and two reflecting pools in the footprints of the original towers. Cascading down the sides will be the largest manmade waterfalls in the country.

– The names of all those who lost their lives on 9/11 will be inscribed on parapets surrounding the reflecting pools.

– It is projected that nine million people will visit downtown each year once construction is finished, thus *what happened on 9/11 will never be forgotten!*

World Trade Center Rendering
(*Image courtesy of dbox / Silverstein Properties, Inc.*)

Acknowledgments

Acknowledgments

Besides recognizing the people who have told their stories in these pages, we want to thank all the others who worked with them. Special thanks go to Rebecca Paley and Kyle Pope who conducted the interviews for this book, wrote them up and edited them. Additionally, Zagat editor Jeff Freier, designers Brian Albert and Jasmine Núñez, and production director Susan Kerutis worked tirelessly on this project. From NYC & Company there were many people, particularly Cristyne Nicholas and Jon Tisch, who deserve recognition for having devoted endless hours to rebuilding the city's tourism businesses. The same can be said of the Partnership for New York City headed, then and now, by Kathy Wylde. Of course, we appreciate Mayor Bloomberg who took office three and a half months after 9/11. His administration inherited many of the aftereffects of the attacks and did a brilliant job of rebuilding the city spiritually and structurally. Finally, thanks go to my assistant, Angela Park, and to my wife, Nina, for putting up with me in this process.